RIOT
South Shields 1930

This play was first produced by The Customs House, South Shields From Monday October 24 to Friday October 28, 2005 and revived at The Customs House and Unity Theatre in Liverpool in summer 2008 by Cloud Nine Theatre Productions, sponsored by the trade union UNISON.

Peter Mortimer is a playwright, poet, editor and peripatetic writer who lives in Cullercoats, North Tyneside. He has written more than twenty plays, several travel books, and three collections of poetry. Five Leaves has previously published three of his books, *I Married the Angel of The North* (Poetry), *Off the Wall: the Journey of a Play* and *The Last of the Hunters: Life with the Fishermen of North Shields*.

For further details, see www.petermortimer.co.uk

Cloud Nine was set up on North Tyneside in 1997, and is committed to new writing from northern playwrights. It has brought to the stage new work from more than twenty dramatists, and also runs a community wing, The Sixties Group, producing work for and by people aged sixty and over. For more details see www.cloudninetheatre.co.uk.

RIOT
South Shields 1930

A Stage Play by
Peter Mortimer

Arabic translation by
Abdulalem Alshamery

Five Leaves Publications
www.fiveleaves.co.uk

RIOT

was published in 2008 by
Five Leaves Publications,
PO Box 8786, Nottingham NG1 9AW
www.fiveleaves.co.uk
info@fiveleaves.co.uk

Copyright © Peter Mortimer 2005
Translation copyright © Abdulalem Alshamery
(of Yemen Voice - theyemenvoice@yahoo.com) 2008
Cover image: Cloud Nine/ARTS UK

ISBN: 978 1 905512 49 2

Five Leaves acknowledges financial support
from Arts Council England

Five Leaves is a member of Inpress
(www.inpressbooks.co.uk),
representing independent publishers

Typeset and design by
Four Sheets Design and Print Ltd
Printed in Great Britain

Arabic cover design: Waleed Fikri

Foreword

A playwright is not by trade an historian, nor a sociologist and the writing of a play is a journey into the unknown — final destination unclear.

When Customs House director Ray Spencer offered me a commission to write a play based round the little-known Yemeni seamen's riot in South Shields on August 2, 1930, at first I declined, being unsure as to where I'd start. I then accepted but was still unsure. I thrashed around for a while during which time people told me not to stir things up. With enough racial tension in the country, and post 9/11, I should forget the play, and let sleeping dogs lie, for we were looking at a direct Muslim/West confrontation. Dropping the whole idea was tempting.

I finally decided to travel to Yemen and persuaded the Arts Council England North-East to give me a travel award. Official government advice was not to visit this dangerous country, a supposed nest of al Qaeda. Like a lot of government advice, this was tosh. I didn't know what I was looking for, and when I got back, I didn't know if I'd found it. The journey affected me so much I wrote a book about it, as well as a play (*Cool for Qat — A Yemeni Journey*).

Bit by bit, over two years, through reading, travelling, making personal contact, and imagining, I added pieces to the Yemeni jigsaw puzzle. I was dealing with a piece of history mostly forgotten in Britain and in Yemen. Yet this painful and at times shameful history had taught the town of South Shields a lesson which I think it hasn't forgotten.

South Shields is probably now among the most racially harmonious towns in the UK, and I submit that the incidents of August 2, 1930 have their part to play in this state of affairs, and for that reason if no other, it is legitimate territory for a playwright to travel in. Plus which historical plays only really work for me if they have a contemporary relevance, and the events of that time resonated loud and clear down the decades during the writing process.

Since the play was first produced in October 2005, the riot and the South Shields Yemeni population in general have received a higher profile. The BBC TV series *Coast* featured the riot, and the recent exhibition at The Baltic, Gateshead, The Last of the Dictionary Men, about the Shields' Yemeni population and history received a good deal of publicity.

I've made every character up, though every character also has some basis in reality and is informed by the events of the time. The play is political, but also personal, with a love story at its heart, because playwrights often start with the big issues but are then pulled towards character, which is as it should be. One of a writer's tasks should be to bring his or her own small illumination to a dark world. Certainly the whole Yemeni experience brought illumination to me, and if a part of it rubs off on you, then my 'umble job is done.

Riot was first performed in October 2005, and in 2008 it is revived at the Customs House as a Cloud Nine production. It also plays at the Liverpool Arab Arts Festival, as part of that city's Capital of Culture celebrations. The director is once again Darren Palmer, himself a third generation South Shields Yemeni, whose grandfather was involved in the Seamen's Minority Movement at the time of the riot. We are pleased to be using several of the original cast.

The play quotes directly from letters in *The Shields Gazette*, quotes are also used from an editorial in *The Seaman*, the magazine of the National Union of Seamen, from speeches by members of the Seamen's Minority Movement and from appeal letters written by Yemeni sailors for financial aid, and the official replies thereto. The boiler-stoking description is taken directly from the book *The Men of the Merchant Service*, by F.T. Bullen (Smith Elder & Co., 1900).

For the best description of the history of the Yemeni population in South Tyneside, I strongly recommend,

From Ta'izz to Tyneside, by Richard I. Lawless (University of Exeter Press, 1995).

And if you see the play in South Shields, when you walk through the theatre's front door, you will almost certainly have just trodden on Mill Dam square, where the riot took place.

Peter Mortimer
Cullercoats, May 2008

Cast List

(In order of appearance).

Yussuf	*A young Yemeni seaman*
Sharp*	*A street fighter manager*
Harry*	*A fight promoter*
News vendor	*A news vendor/masseuse/barber/ barman & the play's Everyman*
Passer-by*	*A passer-by*
George Charlton	*A South Shields ex-seaman*
Thelma	*His daughter*
Margaret	*His wife*
Charters	*An executive of the Shipping Federation*
Ellis	*Secretary of the National Union of Seamen*
Ali Hassan	*A South Shields boarding house master*
Functionary*	*A clerical functionary*
Geordie lad*	*A drunken Geordie lad*
Seamen*	*Two Shields seamen on board ship*
Naval officer*	*A 19th century British naval officer*
Magnate*	*A 19th century shipping magnate*
Trimdon*	*A political activist, member of Seamen's Minority Movement*
Official*	*Foreign Office official*
PC*	*A police constable*
Extras	*Various extras for riot scene, street fight scenes and political speeches scenes*

Parts marked with an asterisk can be tackled by two actors combined.

ACT ONE

The play takes place in South Shields 1929-1930, and briefly in the Gulf of Aden, in the 19th century.

(ENTER YUSSUF. HE IS SPARRING IN A VERY PHYSICAL WAY. ENTER ONE SIDE OF STAGE SHARP, THE OTHER SIDE HARRY).

Sharp: Best fighter we've seen in Shields for years.

Harry: A bloody Arab, street fighting?

Sharp: That lad's poetry in motion.

Harry: Aye, and he keeps taking the prize money Sharp.

Sharp: That's what winners do, they take the prize money. That's why I like managing them.

Harry: He's probably sending it all back to bloody Aden or wherever it is he comes from.

Sharp: What's the matter Harry, running out of competition for my lad?

(ENTER NEWS VENDOR SELLING PAPERS).

News vendor: Extra! Extra! Read all about it! South Shields MP Chuter Ede campaigns for new bridge over the Tyne! Brand new Binns department store opens in King Street! Extra! Extra! *(NOTICES OTHERS).* Hey, you two, off the stage, you're jumping the gun a bit here. The story's not even started yet. The poor lad's only just arrived in Shields *(EXIT SHARP & HARRY).* Come on son *(HELPS YUSSUF GET INTO HIS TRADITIONAL YEMENI GEAR).* There you go. Now then — South Shields 1929, and this lad's a long way from home. A tough town South Shields. Police check every pub for a fight on a Saturday night. And if there isn't one, they start one. Alright son? You'd best find your way to where you're going. Good luck.

9

(EXIT NEWS VENDOR. YUSSUF EVENTUALLY STOPS A PASSER-BY).

Yussuf: Please?

Passer-by: What's that bonny lad?

Yussuf: I want to find —

Passer-by: Speak up son, I cannot make you out.

(YUSSUF SHOWS HIM PIECE OF PAPER. PASSER-BY READS IT).

West Holborn you're after eh? Aye, well I suppose it would be. It's up that way man. Past the Mill Dam and keep to the river. You cannot miss West Holborn. It's a bit of a mucky place, like.

Yussuf: Mr Ali Hassan.

Passer-by: What's that like?

Yussuf: I look for Mr Ali Hassan.

Passer-by: Wouldn't know any Ali Hassan. But then I wouldn't, would I? Where you from then?

Yussuf: Sorry?

Passer-by: No need to be sorry son. Where do you come from?

Yussuf: I come from Yemen.

Passer-by: Yemen eh? Dead hot in Yemen, I bet. Lots of Yemenis in Shields now. Too many, some say.

Yussuf: I am sorry, I —

Passer-by: Not me of course. Live and let live, that's what I say. As long as everyone knows their place. Alright now are you son?

Yussuf: Alright?

Passer-by: Just keep along the river. River Tyne that is son. One of the most famous rivers in the world. You'll not have anything like the River Tyne in Yemen, I bet.

Yussuf: No, I —

Passer-by: Keep close to the river son, you'll be in West Holborn before you know it. *(EXIT BOTH)*.

(MUSLIM MUSIC. POSSIBLY CALL TO PRAYER. SLOWLY FADES AND JACK HYLTON ORCHESTRA SOUND TRACK COMES UP. ENTER THELMA DANCING WITH A CUSHION. DANCES FOR A WHILE. ENTER DAD, GEORGE CHARLTON WHO WALKS WITH A LIMP. HE TURNS OFF MUSIC).

Thelma: Dad!

George: A bloody racket.

Thelma: That's the Jack Hylton Orchestra, dad!

George: I've heard farts more musical than that lot. *(ENTER MUM, MARGARET)*.

Margaret: Let Thelma have her music George.

George: You call that music?

Thelma: It's all the rage down the dance hall.

George: How come she's all tarted up anyway?

Margaret: Thelma's going out, aren't you Thelma?

Thelma: I'm going dancing.

George: Dancing?

Thelma: You don't expect me to stay in here every night do you?

George: You could stay at home and help your mother.

Margaret: It's alright George, I don't need any help.

George: Did you get my Brown? *(MARGARET OPENS A BOTTLE FOR HIM)*.

11

Margaret: I got you three bottles. One and three pence.

George: Don't worry, I'll drink as slowly as I can.

Margaret: I didn't mean that, I —

George: A man's one pleasure in life *(DRINKS)* Even if he can't afford to buy them himself. Anyway, she shouldn't be going out all the time like this.

Thelma: I want some excitement. Not that there's much of that in Shields *(DANCES AGAIN WITH CUSHION)*.

George: Be some lad then is it?

Margaret: Is it Thelma? Some young man?

Thelma: Have you seen most of the lads round here?

(ENTER NEWS VENDOR WHO BEGINS TO DANCE WITH HER).

News vendor: Someone to sweep you off your feet, is that it?

Thelma: Oh yes!

News vendor: A dark stranger full of mystery and passion.

Thelma: You have a way with words newspaper vendor.

(NEWS VENDOR GOES BACK TO HIS JOB).

News vendor: Late night Final! Extra! Extra! Graf Zeppelin arrives in America! 100,000 greet air ship in New Jersey! Read all about it! *(SELLS ONE TO DAD)*.

George: I knew excitement once.

News vendor: You did?

George: Half way round the world and back. Big ships, little ships, merchant navy, Royal Navy. Much bloody good it did me. The only ship I've got now is that one *(INDICATES A MODEL SHIP HE IS BUILDING)*.

12

News vendor: The crossword's on page four.

(EXIT. DAD LEFT ON STAGE TO LOOK AT HIS BOAT.
NEWS VENDOR SETS UP NEXT SCENE FOR CHARTERS
AND ELLIS WHERE CHARTERS IS MAKING A SPEECH).

Charters: Get a move on son, you need a firework up your arse.

News vendor: Sorry sir. There we are sir.

Charters: I'd just like to say in conclusion ladies and gentlemen, as an executive of the Shipping Federation I am not unaware of the present economic woes of the country. It is still only a few years since we suffered the madness and damage of the General Strike, and as such it is time for the whole country to tighten its belt. I would like to say how much at the Federation we appreciate the offer from the National Union of Seamen to take a pay cut of £1 a week for its members. We all have to make sacrifices, so thank you Mr Ellis, thank you *(ACKNOWLEDGES ELLIS)*. And thank you all. If you will excuse me now, I am a very busy man. *(APPLAUSE. CHARTERS STEPS OUT AND SUMMONS NEWS VENDOR)* Waiter?

News vendor: Who me?

Charters: Get this table laid and get some grub out.

(NEWS VENDOR NOW PUTS ON WAITER'S JACKET AND
BRINGS OUT TABLE WITH POSH FOOD ON IT AND A
BOTTLE OF WINE. ELLIS COMES FORWARD).

Ellis: Very fine speech Mr Charters.

Charters: A man does his bit Ellis *(DRINKS)* Waiter! This wine is corked. You'd think at these prices they could provide a wine that didn't taste like pig's piss. A good job it's not coming out of my pocket.

News vendor: May I recommend the Chateauneuf du Pape 1925 vintage sir?

Charters: You wouldn't know a good wine from a glass of vomit, so shut your bloody trap. Just tell the head waiter to bring me something I won't spit out, or he's in trouble.

News vendor: Yes sir. Sir is too kind *(EXITS)*.

Charters: Now then Ellis, man to man there's something I want to say to you. Arabs.

Ellis: Arabs Mr Charters?

Charters: Aye. And lots of them. Cardiff, Liverpool, South Shields, name your port. A lot of them in your Union too.

Ellis: The National Union of Seamen is open to all nationalities.

Charters: Aye. Ever heard of crimping Ellis?

Ellis: I believe I have yes.

Charters: Them bloody Arab boarding house masters. Bribing the officials to get Arabs work on the boats. It's a bloody disgrace. And all them Arabs shipping out through Aden claiming to be British. No more British than the Queen of Sheba most of them.

(ENTER NEWS VENDOR).

News vendor: Actually, that's where she came from.

Charters: Ye what?

News vendor: The Queen of Sheba — she came from Yemen.

Charters: Where's that wine you impudent young bastard?

News vendor: Right here sir.

(POURS GLASS. CHARTERS TASTES IT).

Charters: It's just about passable. *(DURING NEXT PART*

HE SHOULD BE EATING HEARTILY) The thing is this Ellis; A lot of good decent people in this country are going hungry at the moment. Do you know why that is?

Ellis: Hard times. A depression in the USA. The Wall Street crash.

Charters: More and more people looking for fewer and fewer jobs. Take our industry. Excess capacity. And some people say that those who should be getting the jobs aren't getting the jobs.

Ellis: I am not sure I get your drift Mr Charters.

Charters: You tell him Waiter. If you've got a brain that is.

News vendor: I think what Mr Charters is trying to say, now that he's got a decent bottle of wine is that too many Arabs are getting jobs.

Charters: You're a crude bugger aren't you? What's for pudding?

News vendor: We've got spotted dick and custard, bakewell tart, home made apple pie and fresh cream or knickerbocker glory ice cream.

Charters: Actually I'm pretty full. Not sure I could eat another mouthful.

News vendor: Go on sir, force yourself, you can do it!

Charters: Aye well, alright. I'll have spotted dick and to hell with it.

News vendor: See sir? I was right!

Charters: Have you ever wondered Ellis, who the Great British public blame for our economic woes?

Ellis: Well they certainly can't blame the National Union of Seamen, that's one thing.

Charters: Nor should they attach any blame to the likes

of the Shipping Federation. But when you deny a man a square meal, he wants to know whose fault it is.

News vendor: Enjoying your meal Mr Charters?

Charters: I've had better. Think about it Ellis.

News vendor: Will there be anything more sir?

Charters: I think we can safely say everyone's had about enough of you.

(NEWS VENDOR NOW CLEARS AWAY. ELSEWHERE YUSSUF COMES INTO ALI HASSAN'S BOARDING HOUSE. THEY MEET: YUSSUF SHIVERS.THIS SCENE SHOULD BE IN ARABIC).

Ali: You are cold. *(YUSSUF NODS)* This is England. Everything cold here. Weather, blood. The British are a cold race.

Yussuf: I am British now.

Ali: They do not really believe a British skin can be black. You play Blut Yussuf? *(YUSSUF SHAKES HIS HEAD)* It is a very good card game and we play it all the time in the boarding house. Do you have any money? *(YUSSUF PRODUCES YEMENI MONEY)* Your rhials are no good here. Look at this *(IN ENGLISH)* English money.

Yussuf: *(IN ENGLISH)* English money! *(LOOKS AT IT. BACK TO ARABIC)* Thank you.

Ali: Do not thank me. It is not a gift. This is England. Nobody gives anybody anything. It will come out of your wages — if you get any.

Yussuf: *(EXCITED)* England!

Ali: You need to get out of those Yemeni clothes.

Yussuf: What?

Ali: It's better not to look conspicuous here. I have some clothes you can wear.

16

Yussuf: England!

Ali: My advice to you is to stay close to the river and Holborn. Do not stray, and do not cause any bother. Things are not good here at the moment.

Yussuf: What things?

Ali: All in good time. I will show you your room. You have to share it with three other Yemenis. Sometimes more.

Yussuf: *(LOOKS AGAIN AT POUND NOTE AND SPEAKS IN ENGLISH)* English money!

Ali: You are young and you are impulsive Yussuf. That may get you into trouble in South Shields.

Yussuf: South Shields not like Maqbanah.

Ali: Like I say, do not be conspicuous. You must be like everyone else.

Yussuf: Like everyone else?

Ali: That is what I say.

Yussuf: Like everyone else?

Ali: This is an electric light. It switches on and off here. Always put it off when you leave the room empty. You wish to work on the ships?

Yussuf: Yes.

Ali: It is not easy. It is my job to look after you, feed you, shelter you. Any money you earn will come to me as your boarding house master and I take from it what you owe me. You must be patient. Any problems you come to me, you understand?

Yussuf: Yes.

Ali: That is how things are. You will be a good Muslim eh?

Yussuf: In English clothes?

Ali: You have a lot to learn.

Yussuf: Like Blut?

(SHOWS BY HIS ACTIONS THAT THE CLOTHES SEEM STRANGE TO HIM. ENTER NEW VENDOR).

News vendor: Mr Hassan there, he's just trying to keep the peace.

Yussuf: I did not come to England to play Blut.

News vendor: Time was they were crying out for you Arabs to work the ships out of Shields. Times change. Now a lot them would prefer it if you just went home. Toodle pip, tara, auf wiedersehen, arevederci, sling your hook, get my drift?

Yussuf: I cannot understand a single word of that.

News vendor: Fair enough. Hang on. Got to sell a few papers. Extra! Extra! Read all about it! Mauretania breaks her Atlantic crossing record by four hours! Fails to capture the Blue Riband from the German vessel The Bremen! Late night final! Extra! *(SHOWS PAPER TO YUSSUF)* The *Shields Gazette* son. Bastion of free speech, upholder of democracy, oldest evening newspaper in the whole of Great Britain, and not a bad place to buy a second hand bicycle. Plus which it boasts a very lively letters page. Try this one for size.

Dear Editor,
A very big reduction would be made in the number of unemployed if white men were given preference on British ships. At the present times there must be thousands of Arabs, Lascars and Chinamen doing the work on vessels that could be done by our own unemployed. There must be hundreds of Arabs sailing out from our town alone. What makes matters worse is the fact that the majority of these men send every half penny that they possibly can back to Aden or wherever it is they hail from so that the town and country at

large gain nothing from their presence but on the contrary lose to the extent of having to keep the unemployed and their families on the money that could be spent in the town by white firemen and their dependants.

Signed — a Collier.

That's someone who works down a mine by the way. Going to try and register are you?

Yussuf: Register?

News vendor: To be a fireman. On the boats. May as well give it a shot. It's the official way. Hang on. Oye! *(SUMMONS)* Menial functionary! Step this way please! *(HELPS HIM ON WITH HIS DESK AND CLERICAL GEAR)* Pen pushing all day. Pretty boring eh?

Menial functionary: For some of us it brings a certain fulfilment.

News vendor: Fine. A Young able-bodied seamen wishes to register for work.

Menial functionary: Name?

Yussuf: Yussuf Abdullah Kuresh.

Menial functionary: Nationality?

Yussuf: Eh — British!

Menial functionary: Country of birth?

Yussuf: Yemen.

Menial functionary: Place of Birth?

Yussuf: Maq —

News vendor: Aden!

Menial functionary: MacAden?

News vendor: He was born in Aden.

Yussuf: Was I?

Menial functionary: British passport.

Yussuf: What?

Menial functionary: Are you in possession of a British Passport?

News vendor: He is not. No available birth certificate. You know how it is in Yemen.

Menial functionary: *(WRITES DOWN)* "No… passport…" PC5?

Yussuf: What?

Menial functionary: Are you in possession of the PC5 form which enables you to register for work?

Yussuf: I —

News vendor: How can he afford to purchase the PC5 form until he has earned some money?

Menial functionary: *(WRITES DOWN)* No… PC5 form…

Yussuf: I start work straight away?

Menial functionary: File under "Pending Further Information." Good day *(EXIT MENIAL FUNCTIONARY)*.

Yussuf: What is all this?

News vendor: Mr Hassan can fix things, eh Mr Hassan *(ENTER ALI)*.

Ali: Maybe. It is not easy now. Be patient Yussuf. Stay in the boarding house. I shall do what I can.

News vendor: Thanks. Now clear off. There's someone more interesting approaching.

(EXIT ALI. ENTER THELMA DRESSED UP TO GO TO A DANCE. SHE WALKS PAST YUSSUF AND STOPS FOR A MOMENT. EACH IS OBVIOUSLY ATTRACTED TO THE OTHER. THE TWO CLOCK ONE ANOTHER BEFORE

THELMA GOES OFF TO THE DANCE HALL. DANCE MUSIC).

Thelma: It takes me back this music. I'm somewhere exotic and this stranger comes up to me and says *(ENTER GEORDIE LAD)*.

Geordie lad: Fancy a pale ale pet?

Thelma: What?

Geordie lad: I'll buy you a pale ale.

Thelma: A pale ale? Do you find it all grey here?

Geordie lad: How do you mean?

Thelma: The sky, the river, the sea, the people. They've even got a big statue in the centre of Newcastle. Earl Grey.

Geordie lad: Do you not fancy a pale ale then?

Thelma: Do you not ever fancy escaping?

Geordie lad: How do you mean, like?

Thelma: Getting away from all this.

Geordie lad: I've just come in, man.

Thelma: Do you fancy me Geordie lad?

Geordie lad: I reckon I might, aye.

Thelma: You want to marry me, give me lots of babies so I can be elbow deep in nappy suds for the next ten years, is that it?

Geordie lad: You say some funny things, you *(N.V COMES OVER. EXIT GEORDIE LAD)*.

News vendor: I think you fancied him *(INDICATES WHERE YUSSUF WAS)*.

Thelma: He looked a bit different.

News vendor: Mixing with Arabs? What would your dad say?

Thelma: What does he always say? *(ENTER GEORGE)*.

George: Have you any idea what it was like when the Invincible went down, taking 1000 men with it? And just a few of us clinging to the wreckage like drowning rats, slowly freezing to death and me with a piece of metal in my leg the size of a dinner plate? *(ENTER MARGARET)*.

Margaret: Come on George, I'll make you a cup of tea.

George: Then coming home to what? Fighting for your country for what? No work, no future.

Margaret: Yes George.

Thelma: He gets in these moods, see. It's frightening.

George: Not that any bugger cares. And bloody Shields awash with Arabs taking our jobs *(GOES TO HIS MODEL BOAT)* This must be the only boat in Shields with no Arab on it.

Thelma: A bit like one of those gramophone record sometimes.

News vendor: Not like Jack Hylton though.

Thelma: No, not like him. And look at me mam. She's had no life with him. Don't know how she sticks it.

Margaret: *(TO NEWS VENDOR)* It's not his fault. He doesn't understand. Sometimes I don't understand.

Thelma: There she goes again. Always excusing him.

News vendor: Not too much sugar in the tea mind. It's bad for you.

Margaret: Not as bad as his Newcastle Brown. Now don't you be late our Thelma.

Thelma: I might get abducted. I might get carried off to some distant land.

Margaret: No later than ten. You've got work in the morning.

Thelma: I can't wait. *(TO NEWS VENDOR)* Have you ever spent all day every day surrounded by linen bedding?

News vendor: I've lived a sheltered life.

Thelma: Double size sheets, 7/7d per sheet. Pillows extra. Sometimes the excitement gets too much.

Margaret: Your dad will have gone to bed.

Thelma: *(GOES INTO DANCE WITH VARIOUS IMAGINARY PARTNERS).*

So what do you do then? Oh work down the pit. How about you then? Palmers Yard. Yeah. You're a nice looking lad, so what do you dream about? Raich Carter scoring a hat-trick at Roker Park? Got you. What about you bonny lad? Oh dear, he's fallen down drunk. Highly attractive. You have to admire a man who can down ten pints of bitter. Well actually, he can't. And I don't. Admire him, that is.

News vendor: Excuse me. Work calls. Extra! Extra! Read all about it! Extra! Armistice Day! The nation honours its dead! Politicians make pledge never to repeat the futility of war! *(GOES INTO LAUGHTER)* Sorry. I can't help it. A pledge never to repeat the futility of war. The only pledge you could trust them with is the furniture polish!

Thelma: I could be a politician. I could be Prime Minister.

News vendor: A bit Ahead of your time dear. Mind, enter Miss Margaret Bonfield, Minister of Labour and first women cabinet minister.

Thelma: Where?

News vendor: She couldn't make it. Now, you know the rules, get wed, get cooking, get cleaning, get breeding.

Thelma: You like to wind people up.

News vendor: What, like a clock?

Thelma: What about that Arab lad, where is he now?

News vendor: Kicking his heels for three months in the boarding house. There he is look. Playing Blut and chewing qat.

(GO INTO BOARDING HOUSE. YUSSUF JUMPS UP).

Yussuf: *(ARABIC)* I must get work Mr Hassan!

Ali: I am doing all I can.

(WE SEE ALI SEVERAL TIMES OFFER MONEY TO OFFICIAL AND SIGNIFY YUSSUF. ALWAYS OFFICIAL SHAKES HIS HEAD. FINALLY HE TAKES THE MONEY).

Yussuf, at last I have some work for you on a boat as a fireman. Allah be with you.

(YUSSUF NOW TAKES UP THE ROLE OF A FIREMAN SHOVELLING COAL INTO THE BOILER).

News vendor: *(TO THELMA)* Read this have you?

(STARTS READING FROM ARTICLE IN BOOK. HALF WAY THROUGH THELMA TAKES OVER).

"The operator must stand very close to the furnace mouth and peer in at the ferment glow while he searches for the vitals of his fire as quickly and as deftly as may be, lest the tell-tale gauge shall reveal to the watchful engineer the presence of the steam is lessening."

Thelma: But this is only the merest child's play to cleaning fires. When the time comes, the other furnace or furnaces (each fireman has two or three under his charge) must be at the top of their blast, doing their

24

very upmost. Then the fireman flings wide the door of the furnace to be cleaned, plunges his tool into the heart of the fire and thrusts and rakes and slices till he presently, half roasted, drags out into the stokehold floor a mass of clinker *(NEWS VENDOR TAKES BOOK)*.

News vendor: This sends out such a fierce upward heat that it needs must be dampened down,the process being accompanied by clouds of suffocating steam and smoke *(BOOK GOES BACK TO THELMA)*.

Thelma: But there is no time to be lost. Again and again he dives into the heart of the furnace each time purging it of some of the deadening clinker until at last, with smarting eyeballs, half-choked, half-roasted and wholly exhausted for the time, he flings a shovelful of coal upon the by now comparatively feeble fire and returns to call up all his reserves of strength.

(YUSSUF COLLAPSES AT THE END. THELMA MOVES TO GO INTO THE SCENE BUT IS PULLED BACK BY NEWS VENDOR).

News vendor: It is called the dignity of labour — and it's worse than selling bedsheets *(TWO WHITE SEAMEN ENTER)*.

Seaman 1: Here, Arab boy, wash these clothes for me *(SHOVES BUNDLE OF CLOTHES AT YUSSUF WHO SHOVES THEM BACK)*.What's this, a bloody bolshy Arab? See that, this Arab's got ideas above his station. He doesn't want to wash a white man's clothes. Cheeky black bastard.

(FIGHTS YUSSUF WHO KNOCKS HIM DOWN).

Seaman 1: You'll regret that Arab *(BOTH SQUARE UP TO HIM)*.

Thelma: Yussuf! *(AGAIN ATTEMPTS TO GO IN. AGAIN NV PREVENTS HER)*.

Seaman 2: It's your lucky day Arab. If we told the skipper you'd be finished on this boat. So we'll settle it this way, eh?

(BOTH MEN NOW SET ABOUT HIM AND DOWN HIM. EXIT SEAMEN. THELMA BURSTS INTO SCENE AND COMFORTS HIM. NEWS VENDOR LEADS HER OFF AS CHARTERS ENTERS).

Charters: Waiter! (ENTER NEWS VENDOR).

News vendor: Who me?

Charters: Get yourself smartened up and bring me the menu. *(NEWS VENDOR DONS WAITER GEAR AND TAKES MENU TO CHARTERS)* Well, what would you recommend?

News vendor: I'm told that the lamb's liver in mustard sauce with mash and boiled bacon is particularly nice.

Charters: Right — I'll steer well clear of that then. What's the rabbit like?

News vendor: Much slower than it used to be.

Charters: What?

News vendor: It's off the bone, casseroled with carrots and turnips and served with cranberry sauce and a very big smile.

Charters: Are you taking the piss?

News vendor: What, and risk missing my very large tip?

Charters: I'll have the steak and kidney pie. And send that Ellis fellow from the National Union of Seamen in.

News vendor: How would you like him sir, lightly barbecued, roasted or grilled?

Charters: You should be on the stage you clever little shite.

26

News vendor: Oh but I am *(BRINGS ON ELLIS)* Here he is sir.

Ellis: You wanted to see me Mr Charters?

Charters: Ellis, I'm a great fan of that union newspaper of yours, what's it called?

Ellis: The Seaman.

Charters: Rather an unfortunate title if you ask me. No matter. I hear it's an influential organ.

News vendor: Seaman — organ. Blimey!

Ellis: It's read by all our members.

News vendor: And now it's members!

Charters: Patriotic is it Ellis? Stands up for its country?

News vendor: Stands up! Whatever next!

Charters: Eh, you, Mister Smut! Just put a sock in it, right? Ellis, I think it's time this fruitful co-operation between your union and the Shipping Federation reached a new plateau. It's time we stood united and made our position clear. Do you agree?

Ellis: It depends what you had in mind.

Charters: What I had in mind was an editorial in that union newspaper making people aware of what's going on. Make them sit up and think, eh? Isn't that what a free press is for? And you Ellis, as chief man in that union should write that editorial.

News vendor: *(BRINGS IN FOOD)* Enjoy your meal sir.

Ellis: I'm still not sure *(CHARTERS MOTIONS TO HIM AND SPEAKS CONFIDENTIALLY TO HIM)* You don't think that might be a bit provocative Mr Charters?

Charters: I'd call it strategic myself. I'd call it insurance.

Ellis: But in a way it's attacking our very own members.

Charters: Sometimes you have to be fearless, eh? Now let's see just how good a writer you are. *(PROVIDES PEN AND PAPER. ELLIS WRITES THE EDITORIAL AND HANDS IT TO CHARTERS VIA NEWS VENDOR)* Very good Ellis. Do have a boiled spud.

News vendor: Maybe I should read that out Mr Charters. You've got enough on your plate with all that steak pie.

Charters: Very well. Nice and clear now.

Naval officer: *(AS HE READS THIS THE CHARACTERS FROM THE PLAY MOVE IN TO LISTEN)* "It must be understood that we have no kick with the Arabs as such, but charity begins at home and with the elimination of these men who would be better off in the country of their birth, employment would not only be found for our own at present redundant firemen, but room could be found for ex-miners and ex-naval ratings of which so many will be available, especially of the latter, for if the disarmament programmes are carried out, these men will add their quota to the already difficult problem of unemployment."

Charters: A good turn of phrase if I may say so.

George: Bloody good sense that.

Ali: But this makes things worse for all Arab seamen!

Charters: *(TO NEWS VENDOR)* And as for you. You might be so good as to supply a clean pudding spoon. This one's a bloody disgrace *(EXITS WITH HIS ARM ROUND ELLIS)*. An excellent thing the free press Ellis. I think.

News vendor: Extra, extra! Read all about it! Norwegian vessel grounded on the Black Midden rocks in dense fog — no-one dead!

(THIS TAKES US INTO THE BOARDING HOUSE WHERE THE INMATES ARE PLAYING THE CARD GAME BLUT

AND ALSO CHEWING QAT. THIS SCENE IS SPOKEN IN ARABIC WITH SUBTITLES).

Ali: You are a fool Yussuf!

Yussuf: No!

Ali: If a white seaman asks you to wash their clothes, you wash their clothes.

Yussuf: Not me!

Ali: Yemenis are peaceful people. We do not antagonise others.

Yussuf: You should open your eyes.

Ali: What are you talking about?

Yussuf: You are blind — open your eyes!

Ali: I do my best for all, for all twelve of my seamen.

Yussuf: And what about yourself?

Ali: What do you mean by that? *(TO NEWS VENDOR IN ENGLISH)* What does he mean by that?

News vendor: Maybe he thinks you make a tidy living out of looking after your Arab seamen.

Ali: *(BACK TO ARABIC)* That is disgraceful! You don't respect your elders.

Yussuf: *(TO NEWS VENDOR IN ENGLISH)* Tell him I'm going out!

Ali: *(ENGLISH)* He is not a good Muslim!

Yussuf: *(ENGLISH)* I am a good Muslim, but I am still going out!

Ali: *(ARABIC)* Where would you be without me?

Yussuf: Where am I now? *(YUSSUF LEAVES BOARDING HOUSE. MEETS THELMA IN THE STREET).*

Thelma: How's that eye coming on?

Yussuf: It is healing. Thank you.

Thelma: You're nice and slim.

Yussuf: In Yemen, most people are slim.

Thelma: Lots of lads here have got beer bellies.

Yussuf: Beer bellies?

Thelma: Never mind. My name's Thelma Charlton and I can get you a ten per discount on linen bed sheets at Binns.

Yussuf: What do you say?

Thelma: It doesn't matter. What's your name?

Yussuf: My name is Yussuf Abdullah Kuresh.

Thelma: That's nice. Yemen, eh? You could take me there.

Yussuf: Yemen is bad country. Bad rulers. People very poor. England is my home now.

Thelma: England's finished.What's your book?

Yussuf: It is the *Holy Qura'an*.

Thelma: Is it any good?

Yussuf: It is the word of Allah passed down through his prophet Mohammed.

Thelma: Not like Agatha Christie then?

Yussuf: All Muslims read the *Qura'an*.

Thelma: Most of us read *The Gazette*. Hey, did you know William Boyd was playing in *The Leathernecks* at the Grand Electric this week?

Yussuf: I'm sorry. I do not understand.

Thelma: It's alright Yussuf. Do you come from a town then?

Yussuf: Maqbanah — a place high in the mountains.

Thelma: Sounds nice. I bet there's goats and sheep and pigs.

Yussuf: Goats and sheep yes. And cheese and honey. No pigs.

Thelma: I could just eat some honey high upon a mountain.

Yussuf: It is a very poor life. I come to England for civilisation.

Thelma: Civilisation? Hey — say it again.

Yussuf: What?

Thelma: The name of that place you come from.

Yussuf: Maqbanah.

Thelma: Maqbanah! Still — I bet they haven't got the pictures in Maqbanah.

Yussuf: Pictures?

Thelma: Got the talkies all over now Yussuf. I love Gary Cooper. And Greta Garbo.

Yussuf: You are very beautiful but you talk about strange things.

Thelma: I could take you.

Yussuf: Where?

Thelma: To the pictures! Grand Electric. The Palace.The Pavilion. Me and you. Oh say you'll come.

Yussuf: Me and you. And your parents will be there too?

Thelma: Course not! Look, I want to do this *(KISSES HIM)* Don't you like it?

Yussuf: These things do not happen in Yemen.

Thelma: They don't happen enough in Shields come to that. Except with blokes who slaver and slurp Bass

31

Blue Label all over you. You could lend me your book.

Yussuf: I cannot lend you the book, no.

Thelma: I could get my own copy then.

Yussuf: The *Qura'an* is for Muslims.

Thelma: Agatha Christie's for anyone *(KISSES HIM AGAIN. MORE RECEPTIVE)*.

Yussuf: Now my head is spinning fast.

Thelma: Mine too. Next week then. We could go for a drink in The Eagle first.

Yussuf: Muslims don't drink.

Thelma: Men who don't drink? You don't get many of them for the pound in South Shields! I wonder what the Qura'an says about dancing? Got any music news vendor?

News vendor: Coming right up! *(MUSIC)*.

Thelma: Come on then *(THEY DANCE)* Dancing is living Yussuf. It's being alive. When I dance, nothing else matters. Hey, you're a natural, you've got rhythm! *(DANCE BRINGS THEM CLOSE)* So, you've never kissed an English girl before?

Yussuf: I have never kissed any girl. Only my mother. And my sister.

Thelma: That's different.

Yussuf: Yes. I like English kissing *(NOW HE KISSES HER)*.

Thelma: Maybe you're a bit of a dark horse — oh, no offence intended of course!

Yussuf: Dark horse?

Thelma: Never mind.

Yussuf: I want to know about everything. Experience

everything.

Thelma: Me too. Maybe you came all the way from Yemen to meet me.

Yussuf: Maybe.

Thelma: Why did you travel all the way from Yemen anyway, just to work in South Shields.

News vendor: Maybe I could be of some assistance there.

Thelma: Oh, it's old know-all. I suppose you know everything?

News vendor: You could say that.

Thelma: Alright — what's the world's second highest mountain then?

News vendor: The mountain is called K2 and it stands at 28,250 ft.

Thelma: Big head.

News vendor: I also know why and how the Yemenis came to work in South Shields.

Thelma: And I suppose you're going to tell us.

News vendor: Picture the scene. It is January 1839. Enter one high-ranking British naval officer *(ENTER OFFICER)*.

Naval officer: You there! Humble naval rating! Smarten yourself up! *(NEWS VENDOR NOW DONS SOMETHING APPROPRIATE TO NAVAL RATING)* Get a move on, come on! Don't want to be keelhauled, do you? Now then, can you see the Port of Aden over there? *(NEWS VENDOR EXITS AND RETURNS WITH A GIANT TELESCOPE)*.

News vendor: *(LOOKING THROUGH IT)* Yes sir! I can see Aden sir!

Naval officer: Part of some country called Yemen I'm told. We need to occupy that port on behalf of the British Crown immediately.

News vendor: Yes sir!

Naval officer: Damned fuzzy wuzzies had the cheek to occupy a stranded British naval vessel. The blighters need to be taught a lesson.

News vendor: Yes sir! Is that the real reason for occupying Aden sir?

Naval officer: What?

News vendor: As I recall sir, it's two years since that vessel was occupied.

Naval officer: Are you being insubordinate?

News vendor: Certainly not sir! God bless Queen Victoria sir, and all who sail in her sir! Just thought I'd mention how Great Britain seriously needs a refuelling station between Bombay and Suez sir, and Aden would seem to fit the bill perfectly sir. Begging your pardon sir.

Naval officer: If you don't want the cat o' nine tails lad, I suggest you keep quiet about things you don't understand.

News vendor: Of course sir I'll occupy Aden straight away sir! Just thought I'd mention sir that some of the lads — not me you understand sir — also think that occupying Aden might be to prevent Egypt from occupying Southern Arabia and becoming a threat to the expansion of Great Britain, sir!

Naval officer: Get on with it! Occupy Aden!

News vendor: Straight away sir! *(DOES IT)* Aden occupied sir! Now British territory *(RUN UP A FLAG ETC)*. Which of course sir now makes everyone born in

Aden entitled to a British passport and citizenship and the benefits accruing there from — sir! Permission sir to move everything on half a century and change you from an imperialistic naval officer into a successful shipping magnate sir!

Naval officer: Very well. Permission granted.

(HE BECOMES A MAGNATE. NEWS VENDOR BECOMES MIDSHIPMAN).

Magnate: So Mr Midshipman, we're short of labour on the boats are we?

News vendor: Aye aye, we are that sir. Business is expanding so fast, we just haven't got enough seamen.

Magnate: Have to find a new source then. Now I hear all those Arabs are pretty hard-working.

News vendor: To a man sir. Hard working and reliable.

Magnate: And sober from what I'm told.

News vendor: They never touch a drop sir.

Magnate: Not like our lot, eh? Pissed as rats half the time the minute they step on shore, and they're still pissed when they return to the ship. If they do return that is. We could do with those Arabs. Plenty of work in Cardiff, Liverpool and South Shields. Those Yemeni chaps — if they sign on in Aden, they can claim British nationality. Makes it all easier.

News vendor: Even if they don't come from Aden?

Magnate: It's only a bloody rule. If they've got any sense, they'll say that they do.

News vendor: Not much experience on ships these Arabs sir.

Magnate: Put 'em to work as firemen. You hardly need to be an admiral to shovel coal into a furnace.

News vendor: Right away sir. Come on then you lads, this way now. That's it. Keep it moving lads. Assalam Alaikum — cracking! Now put your backs into it. *(EXIT MAGNATE AND NEWS VENDOR GOES BACK TO NORMAL. SPEAKS TO THELMA)* Sorry, were you saying something?

Thelma: I was saying how me and Yussuf were going to go to the pictures. You've never been have you Yussuf?

Yussuf: There is so much I have not done.

Thelma: Come on then. *(THEY GO TO THE PICTURES AND SIT DOWN)* See — that's Randolph Scott. He's handsome isn't he? Mind so are you Yussuf. It's that smile of yours. How would you fancy being famous?

Yussuf: You think I could be famous?

(ENTER SHARP SIDE OF STAGE).

Sharp: Why not son? Words got out you're pretty handy with your fists. That bloke you dropped on the ship. Supposed to be a real hard man.

Yussuf: Who are you?

Sharp: The name's Sharp. I'm always on the look-out for a new street fighter.

Yussuf: Street fighter?

Sharp: The blood pit son. Normally quiet little devils the Yemenis. A street fighter might be a novelty. It's good money.

(ENTER OTHER SIDE OF STAGE TRIMDON).

Trimdon: The name's Trimdon brother Yussuf. Recently formed Shields branch of Minority Seamen's Movement. You stood up for workers' rights on that boat.

Yussuf: So?

Trimdon: We fight for seamen's rights, whatever their colour, or nationality. The National Union of Seamen have sold out. I want you to appear on the platform with me at Mill Dam next week. Solidarity.

Thelma: Do you mind, we're watching the film.

Trimdon: More important things in life than films darling.

Thelma: I'm not your darling.

Trimdon: Do you realise the NUS is a right wing reactionary outfit betraying its Arab members and colluding with the ship owners to force them out of work?

Thelma: I realise we're missing the best part of the film.

Sharp: I'll give you a run out son. You keep 40 per cent of your winnings. It's not Queensberry rules, and there's some hard nuts in there. What do you say?

Thelma: I say get lost both of you. We're on a date.

Sharp: What do you say son?

Trimdon: Brother Yussuf?

Yussuf: I —

Thelma: Yussuf.

Yussuf: I came here to see Randolph Scott. And for an English kiss.

(HE KISSES THELMA WHO RESPONDS).

Sharp: Later then, eh?

Trimdon: When the novelty's worn off brother Yussuf.

(EXIT BOTH).

Thelma: Thank you Yussuf. It'll be alright, you'll see.

Yussuf: Yes, it will be alright.

(ENTER NEWS VENDOR. THEY ARE KISSING AGAIN).

News vendor: Extra! Extra! Late Night Final. League of Nations celebrates its tenth anniversary. Read all about it! Public smoking by women — Lady Astor speaks out! Extra! Extra! Oye — you two, the film's finished, time to go home!

(EXIT YUSSUF AND THELMA. NEWS VENDOR LEFT ON STAGE ON HIS OWN. LOOKS ROUND HIM FOR A BIT THEN SUMMONS FROM WINGS).

Oye! Mrs.Charlton — get on here and advance the story if you don't mind *(ENTER MARGARET)*.

Margaret: It doesn't have to be a problem George *(ENTER GEORGE)*.

George: It doesn't have to be a problem? Our Thelma with a bloody Arab?

Margaret: It's her choice.

George: And what's wrong with Shields lads?

Margaret: I don't know, I mean — *(ENTER THELMA)*.

Thelma: I love him dad.

George: Ye what?

Thelma: Yussuf. I love him.

George: That takes the biscuit.

Thelma: You've never met him.

George: I meet him every time I go down to Mill Dam looking for work. I meet him every time they give a job to some Arab and there's nowt for your dad.

Thelma: But you're not well dad and —

George: I'm well enough to work on the boats. I'm as well as any Arab.

Margaret: I don't want you upsetting yourself George.

Thelma: I'm bringing him here.

George: Ye what?

Thelma: To this house. I'm bringing Yussuf. I want him to meet me mam and dad.

George: Bloody hell.

Margaret: Thelma, I'm not sure that's such a good idea and —

Thelma: I'm not ashamed of him mam. I'm proud of him. I'm not hiding him away.

Margaret: Course not pet, but —

George: Bringing an Arab seaman here?

Thelma: You'd better get used to the idea. Both of you.

George: She's gone dotty.

Margaret: Thelma —

Thelma: Now don't you take the easy way out mam, like you always do. You make Yussuf welcome, do you hear? Just for once in your life, don't appease mi dad.

Margaret: I'll have to think about this.

Thelma: Yes mam, why don't you do that?

(EXITS. GEORGE AND MARGARET LOOK AT ONE ANOTHER. FINALLY HE GOES OFF TO HIS MODEL BOAT. ENTER NEWS VENDOR).

News vendor: That model boat of his — it comes from Billy Boy's Workshop in the *Gazette*. That's where he got the idea. One day he might finish it. Don't hold your breath though. Here, Ali, I'll deal the cards for you. A few hands of Blut, eh? Come on Yussuf, concentrate.

Ali: *(TO NEWS VENDOR)* You know how to play Blut?

News vendor: I know everything *(ARABIC)*.

Ali: He keeps getting it wrong, Yussuf —

News vendor: His mind is elsewhere you might say *(ARABIC)*.

Ali: Yes. With that white girl. *(DEALS WHILE HE SPEAKS. OTHERS GATHER ROUND)* You are my partner Yussuf. Come on now. No. No you should have chosen hearts for trumps there. And you have the master card remember, play with your partner.

Yussuf: I am sorry.

Ali: Very well. Play. No. Now hearts are not trumps so the jack of hearts only counts for two, not twenty. Play on.

Yussuf: I am sorry. I love her, but have no money. You can fix it?

Ali: Very little work for Arabs now. The PC5 makes it very difficult. Not always possible.

(YUSSUF LEAPS UP AND WALKS OUT OF THE BOARDING HOUSE. MEETS SHARP. THEY LOOK AT ONE ANOTHER AND WALK OFF TOGETHER. ENTER NEWS VENDOR).

News vendor: Hang on — I've a feeling I'm about to be in demand.

(ENTER CHARTERS. HE IS LATHERED UP READY FOR A SHAVE).

Charters: Now where's that bloody barber?

News vendor: *(PUTTING ON BARBER'S COAT)* Right here sir!

Charters: I want this skin as smooth as a baby's arse, alright? And watch what you're doing with that cut throat *(GETS HIM READY IN THE BARBER'S CHAIR AND STARTS SHAVING HIM)* Come on Ellis *(ENTER*

ELLIS) You could do with a bit of a shave yourself. Get this lad to do it for you. Have it on me.

Ellis: It's the Seamen's Minority Movement Mr Charters.

Charters: What is?

Ellis: They're causing a lot of bother in South Shields. Stirring things up.

Charters: That's what commies always do. That's all they exist for. Bloody hell barber. What was your previous job, a hedge-clipper?

News vendor: I was an undertaker, sir.

Charters: Pull the other one.

News vendor: Dead keen I was. Get it? Mind, I used to get mortal sometimes. Mortal, eh? I'd down a few stiff ones. Stiff ones!

Ellis: They're trying to get all the seamen to boycott the boats, and resist the PC5.

Charters: What, white with Arab?

Ellis: That's what they're saying, yes.

Charters: That would be unfortunate. Mind, I think we've done enough to make sure it doesn't happen. Bloody hell barber, you're not mowing a lawn!

News vendor: Sorry sir.

Charters: Would you say I've got a double chin?

News vendor: Double? Oh no, that's not the word at all sir!

Charters: Anyway Ellis, they'll have more than the PC5 to worry about soon.

Ellis: You mean this new rota system?

Charters: Works well enough in Antwerp I'm told. And

it's being introduced after a full appraisal of the industry and the market.

Ellis: The word is it's being introduced to penalise the Arab seamen.

Charters: Now why would we do that?

Ellis: Longest ashore gets first choice of work. An obvious advantage for white men.

Charters: If you're faced with two angry dogs Ellis, what do you do?

Ellis: Angry dogs?

Charters: Make sure they go for each other's throat and not yours.

Ellis: I've been as co-operative as I can with the Shipping Federation Mr Charters.

Charters: If only more union men were like you. If only this barber didn't have the finesse of an orang-utan.

News vendor: Mrs Charters won't even know you when I'm finished with you sir.

Charters: Aye, a man can dream. How much do you charge for this cut throat butchery anyway?

News vendor: It's very reasonable. You could say it's a snip.

Charters: Bugger off then.

(GETS UP, GIVES NEWS VENDOR SOME MONEY).

News vendor: That's exceedingly unimpressive *(EXITS).*

Charters: Minority Seamen's Movement, protest marches, rallies. If people get angry Ellis, they need a target for that anger. They can feel let down, betrayed. Something's gone wrong. Now what is it? You. *(THIS TO NEWS VENDOR)* Let's have some of that patriotic music!

News vendor: Coming right up!

(THE LIKES OF "THERE WILL ALWAYS BE AN ENGLAND". CHARTERS BRINGS ON DAD WHO IS HOLDING HIS OLD NAVAL UNIFORM).

Dad: I was proud to wear this. Proud to fight for King and Country. Proud to be out on those high seas.

Charters: You're a good man, a fine man.

Dad: I'm a forgotten man.

Charters: Forgotten? No — the country is in your debt.

Dad: Chucked on the scrapheap.

Charters: We do all we can. Look around you. Things change.

Dad: I don't like what I see.

Charters: Men like you. The backbone of this country. Seeing it all taken from you. How hard is it? Seeing others take it all from you?

END OF ACT ONE

ACT TWO

(ENTER NEWS VENDOR).

News vendor: Late Night Final! Channel Tunnel White Paper published! Proposal rejected! Extra! Extra! Where are you off to Yussuf?

(ENTER YUSSUF).

Yussuf: I try for work myself *(GOES TO SIGN ON. ENTER FUNCTIONARY).*

Functionary: Sorry, no work.

Yussuf: Plenty of men signing on for work on the Cape Verde.

Functionary: Sorry.

Yussuf: Plenty of white men. Why not me?

News Vendor: Try this.

(READS FROM SHIELDS GAZETTE).

Dear Editor,

To say that an Arab is equal to a Britisher — I don't know whether to laugh or get mad when I think of it. Why, not even ten per cent of them are British subjects even though they claim to be. As for their bravery during the war, the less said about that, the better; from my own experience and that of my friends, half of the Arabs lost during the war died of fright before the sea got to them. The union was built up by white sailors and firemen and a going concern long before the Arabs came here to deprive white men of work and gain for South Shields the name of Cardiff the second. I'm sure it would not go bankrupt if all the Arabs were out of it. My advice to these gentlemen as they are too thick-skinned to see that they are not wanted, is to get

44

while the going is good. Furthermore, I don't merely dislike Arabs. I hate them. Signed Bugho.

(MAYBE WE GET AN ECHO OF THE LETTER'S LAST SENTENCE. YUSSUF WALKS AWAY AND SEEKS OUT SHARP AND HOLDS OUT HIS HANDS. SHARP CHECKS HIS FISTS AND TELLS HIM TO GET HIS SHIRT OFF. WE HAVE SOME PREPARATION FOR A FIGHT. ENTER HARRY).

Harry: You're putting up an Arab? They cannot fight for toffee, Sharp man.

Sharp: Aye well. Just put your money where your mouth is Harry Walton.

(WE NOW HAVE A WHITE OPPONENT COME FORWARD AND THE FIGHT TAKES PLACE. YUSSUF IS TOO GOOD FOR THE OTHER MAN. OTHER CHARACTERS FROM THE PLAY ACT AS SPECTATORS. AT THE END SHARP PUTS MONEY IN YUSSUF'S HAND. HE AND OTHERS EXIT LEAVING YUSSUF AND THELMA).

Thelma: Is that a cut over your eye? *(SHE LOOKS AT IT. THEY SHARE A TENDER MOMENT).* Do you do this for me Yussuf?

Yussuf: I must be a man for you.

Thelma: You're a man alright. Will you come to my house?

Yussuf: Your house?

Thelma: There'll not be any pork *(ENTER SHARP).*

Sharp: Yussuf.

(ANOTHER FIGHT. SAME PROCEDURE. YUSSUF WINS).

They're queuing up to try to give an Arab a good hammering. You're good for business Yussuf. You're very good for business!

Yussuf: *(TO THELMA)* It will be alright?

Thelma: My dad was a bit — you know. He says he's alright about it now. Me and you Yussuf, how can it not be alright? Hey, you're pretty good.

Sharp: Natural street fighter pet. Like he was born to do it.

Thelma: He was born for me. Him and his — book.

(SHE WATCHES AS HE GOES THROUGH HIS SPARRING ROUTINE. HE SEEMS VERY INTO IT. WHILE THIS IS GOING ON, TRIMDON HAS GOT UP ON A SOAP BOX ELSWHERE ON STAGE AND HAS ATTRACTED MEN AROUND HIM).

Trimdon: Let me read to you brothers from the Tyneside District of the Communist Party of Great Britain. *(READS)* The seamen are fighting this triple alliance of ship-owners, the Labour government and the fascist union of seamen, the NUS. To smash this alliance and win through to victory the seamen must adopt the strong measures and break with the policy of passive resistance. Effective action must be taken to prevent scabs signing on and thus defeating your fight — this cannot be done by passive resistance — no seamen should be allowed into the Shipping Federation or NUS offices until your demands are met by the Shipping Federation and ship-owners. Passive resistance has failed to hold up a single ship and this reveals itself as a useless and dangerous policy. Active prevention of the back legs signing on will hold up all the ships and enable you to declare these ships black and call upon all seamen and dockers in all ports to see these ships get no crews on no dockworkers. *(SPOTS YUSSUF)* Brother Yussuf. Will you join us? Will you fight?

Yussuf: I am fighting *(SPARS HIS WAY OFF STAGE STRAIGHT TOWARDS ALI).*

Ali: White men are getting angry at you Yussuf.

46

Yussuf: Everyone is getting angry.

Ali: Even Yemeni seamen.

Yussuf: I have got to go. I have an important meeting.

*(EXIT ALI. ENTER THELMA. DURING THE NEXT
EXCHANGES YUSSUF GETS READY TO MEET THE
FAMILY).*

Thelma: I'm a bit nervous Yussuf. Are you nervous?

Yussuf: I am fine. Allah will provide.

Thelma: You don't know how much it means to me, me
dad agreeing to see you.

Yussuf: I'm sure your father is a good man.

News vendor: *(ENTERS WITH A BUNCH OF FLOWERS)*
Hey — take these!

Yussuf: What?

News vendor: For Mrs Charlton.

Yussuf: Thank you.

Thelma: It must be nice having a faith Yussuf.

Yussuf: You have no faith?

Thelma: Not many of us bother with church and things.
Weddings, funerals, you know, that's about it. They
smell lovely those flowers. What happened with my dad
was his boat got blown up and sunk in the war. Loads
of men drowned. He got injured and has been limping
ever since. Never been the same, can't get work back on
the Shields boats.

Yussuf: And he blames the Arabs.

Thelma: Sort of. Thanks for coming Yussuf.

Yussuf: I must know everything about you Thelma. I
am a lucky man. In Yemen these things are arranged

47

by others.

Thelma: I couldn't be having that. Kiss me and we'll go in *(THEY KISS AND ENTER THE HOUSE)* Mam? Dad? We're here! *(ENTER DAD)* Oh hello dad. Dad, this is Yussuf, Yussuf this is my dad. *(THEY SHAKE HANDS)* Where's mam?

George: Your mother'll be back soon. She had to go out.

Thelma: Out, but she was expecting us and —

George: She'll not be long. Flowers?

Yussuf: They are for Mrs Charlton.

George: A long time since any bugger bought her flowers. Just stick them down there. She'll put them in water when she gets back. D'ye like a drink Yussuf? A beer?

Thelma: Muslims don't drink dad.

George: I'm sure the lad's got a tongue in his head. Yussuf?

Yussuf: Thank you, no.

George: I see. I'll have a bottle of brown. Newcastle Brown ale. Famous stuff. Ever heard of it? *(POURS HIMSELF A GLASS)*.

Yussuf: Yes, I have.

George: Strong stuff. A man's drink you might say.

Thelma: Dad likes the odd bottle, don't you. In moderation.

George: She worries I might drink too much son. I normally do as well. Sure you won't have one?

Yussuf: No — thank you.

George: Very sociable on Tyneside, a bottle of Brown. It's how men relax with one another.

Thelma: Like I said dad, Muslims don't drink.

George: Aye like you said. So what do you do then?

Yussuf: I am sorry.

George: To relax like, wind down. After a day's work. If there is a day's work.

Yussuf: Yemenis chew qat.

George: Cat? Well I've heard of places where people eat dog, but cat?

Yussuf: No. No Mr Charlton, you do not understand. Qat is a leaf.

George: A leaf? You're saying Yemenis chew leaves — like monkeys?

Thelma: Where exactly is mam, dad?

George: Like I said, your mother had to go out. And like I said, she'll be back before long. She'll have something to eat I'm sure. No pig *(TAKES A DRINK)* One of the finest tastes in the world that lad. The best brewing brains in the country got together to make it. Go on, have a drop.

Yussuf: It is very kind of you Mr Charlton, but no.

George: What would happen if you took a drink then. A thunderbolt come down and strike you, would it?

Yussuf: Alcohol is forbidden.

George: Aye well. What's that you've got with you?

Yussuf: It is my copy of The *Qura'an*.

George: I see. I wonder what you think of this?

(PRODUCES MODEL BOAT).

Yussuf: It is very well made.

George: Got plenty of time to spend on it these days. A man of leisure you might say.

Thelma: Me dad's always been good with his hands, haven't you dad?

George: I've heard your lad's good with his fists. Is that right?

Yussuf: That is very kind of you.

George: Knocked a couple of Shields lads flat already I heard. Can I have a look at your *Qura'an* then?

Yussuf: It is best not to pass the holy book over —

George: Oh come on son, I just want a look, friendly like. No harm in that is there? Is there Thelma?

Thelma: Maybe just let him have a little look Yussuf.

(YUSSUF HANDS OVER THE BOOK BUT RELUCTANTLY).

George: I can't understand it.

Yussuf: It is written in Arabic.

George: Oh Arabic? It's all squiggles to me. Is this the truth then, this book?

Yussuf: The truth?

George: Ye know, I mean if this is the truth, then our *Bible* can't be the truth as well, can it?

Yussuf: Well I —

George: Just like if your Allah is the real God, then ours must be a fake one , mustn't he?

Thelma: Dad can you just leave it and —

George: No, no, your dad's curious about such things. He's not as stupid as you think.

Yussuf: To a Muslim the *Qura'an* is the truth.

George: To a Muslim — right. Like a cup of tea?

Yussuf: That would be very nice.

George: She'll make you one when she gets back. So — you like our Thelma then?

Yussuf: It is more than like.

George: Oh like that is it?

Thelma: We love each other dad.

George: Love — aye. *(PICKS UP BOAT)* You have to be careful with these. Very fragile you see. It looks like the real thing, but it isn't. Just pretend really.

Yussuf: Please Mr Charlton, could I have my *Qura'an* back.

George: Just give us a minute, eh? *(EXAMINES IT)* You should be pleased. Me taking an interest. I've got a *Bible* somewhere in the house. Not that I go in for the hymning and praying nonsense. Do you want to marry Thelma, do you?

Thelma: Dad!

George: It seems a perfectly reasonable question. Well?

Yussuf: I would like to spend all my life with her, yes.

George: You haven't got any other wives tucked away anywhere have you?

Thelma: Can you stop this dad?

George: Polygamy, that's what they call it isn't it, your lot?

Thelma: You sent mother away didn't you?

George: Like I said, she'll be back in a minute.

Thelma: You've set this up. You bastard.

George: You dare call your dad a bastard?

Thelma: You horrible bitter bastard.

George: Oh that's it is it, me to blame, eh?

Yussuf: Please, I do not understand —

George: You keep quiet son. You're a guest in this house. Just like you're a guest in this country. *(TAKES A DRINK. HE IS DRINKING HEAVILY)* Why not have a drink, eh? All calm down, eh? What harm will it do? One small bloody drink? It's not poison you know, it's just bloody Newcastle Brown. You see lad, when I drink, everything seems a bit better. I haven't got this gammy leg. I can think about going down to Mill Dam in the mornings and maybe getting some work. I can think that maybe there is a reason for getting up each day after all, and that England is still England.

Yussuf: I am very sorry for you Mr Charlton.

George: Sorry for me? You? An Arab? Sorry for me?

Yussuf: Perhaps we should go Thelma. It does not feel good here. Please may I have my copy of the *Qura'an* back Mr Charlton?

George: A bloody Arab — sorry for me!

Yussuf: The holy book please *(GOES TO TAKE IT. DAD DOESN'T ALLOW HIM)*.

Thelma: Dad, give him the *Qura'an*.

George: Oh I'm taking orders from my own daughter now am I?

Yussuf: Please Mr Charlton. I do not want any trouble.

George: Oh you hear that? The Arab doesn't want any trouble. He wants to come hear, steal our jobs, seduce our women, make fools out of the lot of us, but he doesn't want any trouble.

Yussuf: Please. Give me the *Qura'an*. I go now.

George: You must think I'm stupid son. Like I don't know what's going on. Fighting for me bloody country, then coming home to find no work and the place is full of bloody wogs. Nice homecoming, eh? And I'm supposed to welcome you into this house am I, wish you all the best with my daughter, your filthy black hands all over her and —

Thelma: Stop it dad!

George: Stop it? Stop him and all the other Arab bastards, coming half way round the world to pinch our jobs and here's me born a few streets away from Mill Dam, and can't get work. Do you know what it's like son, a man without work?

Thelma: You do what you can dad.

George: I do sod all. I'm useless. And it's him that makes me useless. And I'd chuck every one of them out of Shields, send them packing to their bloody mud huts or wherever they came from because they don't belong here.

Yussuf: Please, the book. I go.

George: That's all you're bothered about eh, your sodding book? Never mind whose life is ruined eh? Well this is what I think of your book. *(GOES TO TEAR QURA'AN IN HALF. YUSSUF PICKS UP THE MODEL BOAT AND PREPARES TO WRECK IT. A STAND OFF)* Harm that boat and you're a dead man.

Yussuf: I only want the *Qura'an*. Then I go.

George: True colours eh? Take our jobs, our daughters, then wreck the only thing a man has left. See that Thelma?

Thelma: Just put the book down dad. Please.

George: Tell him to get his filthy Arab hands off that boat.

Thelma: Yussuf?

(AFTER THE STAND-OFF DAD RUSHES YUSSUF, BUT IS

*CLEARLY IN NO CONDITION TO COMPETE. ENTER
MARGARET DURING THE STRUGGLE).*

Margaret: What the —

Thelma: Stop them mam! *(SHE PARTS THEM. BOAT IS
DAMAGED IN THE PROCESS)* Mam, this is Yussuf.

Yussuf: *(PICKS UP BUNCH)* I brought you some flowers
Mrs Charlton.

Margaret: Bloody hell.

Yussuf: You must put them in water. Or they die.

Thelma: He wanted you out the way mam. He wanted a
showdown with Yussuf.

George: This is still my own bloody house.

*(OPENS ANOTHER BOTTLE OF BROWN. HE IS ABOUT
TO TAKE A DRINK WHEN YUSSUF TAKES IT FROM HIM
AND DRINKS IT).*

Yussuf: So now I have become a man, have I, Mr
Charlton? *(DAD SNATCHES THE BOTTLE BACK)* Not
for you, this. For Thelma.

George: I don't want to hear you speak my daughter's
name you Arab bastard. I want you out of this house for
good, and I'll never have her speak your name again
either.

Thelma: You can't just do that dad, I —

George: Is that bloody clear, both of you —

Yussuf: Not all white men are like you.

George: Ye what?

Yussuf: Not all full of hatred *(DAD TRIES TO GO FOR HIM
AGAIN. MARGARET AND THELMA RESTRAIN HIM).*

George: Get out! Get out!

Margaret: Just go son.

Yussuf: I'm sorry Mrs Charlton, I —

Margaret: Just go, eh?

(EXIT YUSSUF. THEY PUT DAD IN A CHAIR).

George: So what are you looking at?

Margaret: I'm looking at you.

George: Get the tea woman. Well? Ye gone deaf or something? *(TO THELMA)* And what are you standing there for gawping like a bloody idiot?

Thelma: Are you going to say anything mother?

George: Why the hell should she say anything?

Thelma: You just going to say nothing then eh?

George: She's got nowt to bloody say man. Have you woman?

Margaret: I have actually.

Thelma: Say it then. I want to hear it. I've always wanted to hear it.

George: So what is it then? This 'thing' you've got to say.

Margaret: I —

George: Spit the bloody thing out woman, then get my tea on!

Margaret: Feeling sorry for yourself all these years.

George: What?

Margaret: Me saying nothing. I'm disgusted with myself as I am with you.

George: Ye bloody what?

Margaret: Nothing's your fault, is it?

George: That's enough *(HITS HER).*

Margaret: *(EVENTUALLY)* Blame it on the war, the

Arabs, anything except yourself. And what about us eh? This family. Me, you and Thelma. I've been weak and foolish, keeping the peace when it's hardly worth keeping.

George: So you're siding with the Arabs now are you woman? They're coming here taking our jobs and —

Margaret: Oh yes — everything's Yussuf's fault. Depression, unemployment, poverty, it's all down to that young Yemeni lad, isn't it?

George: Why you bloody — *(MAKES TO GO TOWARDS HER THREATENINGLY BUT BREAKS DOWN AND CRADLES THE BOAT. ENTER NEWS VENDOR WITH NEWSPAPERS).*

News vendor: Extra! Extra! Read all about it! South Shields thrown out of Football League! Final game at Horsley Hill today! It's goodbye to the seasiders! Extra! Extra! *(TO THELMA)* Are you alright?

Thelma: Alright?

News vendor: Those flowers are wilting.

(DOES SOME BUSINESS WITH FLOWERS, SELLS A NEWSPAPER TO DAD, LEADS THELMA AND MAM OFF STAGE. SPEAKS FINAL SENTENCE TO DAD BEFORE LEADS HIM OFF TOO).

Final fixture against Accrington Stanley you know.

(NEWS VENDOR ALONE ON STAGE. YUSSUF RUSHES PAST IN AGITATED STATE).

News vendor: Whoa! Whoa! Where's the fire.

Yussuf: What?

News vendor: It's not the end of the world.

Yussuf: What do you know?

News vendor: You mean, apart from everything?

(YUSSUF RUNS OFF INTO THE BOARDING HOUSE TO BE MET BY ALI. FOLLOWING SCENE IN ARABIC).

Ali: Yussuf — what is the matter?

Yussuf: Nothing.

Ali: Something is wrong. Come here. *(SMELLS HIS BREATH)* You have been drinking alcohol. This is very bad for a Muslim. Where have you been. *(NO REPLY)* Is this what happens when you go to the house of a white woman?

Yussuf: Her name is Thelma.

Ali: First you are fighting in the streets. Now you are drinking. And your fellow seamen here almost starving.

Yussuf: What?

Ali: We do not know what to do Yussuf. We have joined the Minority Seamen's Movement. We have agreed to boycott the ships. They say it will bring justice.

Yussuf: Justice?

Ali: Of course. You do not understand. You have drunk alcohol. You cannot be in a state of grace. You must leave the boarding house for now.

Yussuf: Leave?

Ali: I have more important things to think about than you. Go.

(EXIT YUSSUF. GOES STRAIGHT TO SHARP).

Yussuf: I am ready.

Sharp: Aye, you look it son.

Yussuf: Where is the man I fight?

Sharp: Here he is *(CROWD GATHERS FOR FIGHT. YUSSUF IS RUTHLESS AND BEATS THE MAN EASILY. SHARP STEPS IN)* That'll do Yussuf. The man's well beat.

Yussuf: Where is the next one?

Sharp: The Maqbana Mauler, eh? All in good time son, all in good time *(OUT LOUD)* Any takers for the Maqbana Mauler?

(YUSSUF IS STILL SPARRING FURIOUSLY, SHADOW BOXING. ENTER THELMA).

Thelma: Yussuf.

Yussuf: Yes.

Thelma: I'm so sorry Yussuf.

Yussuf: I am sorry too.

Thelma: I didn't want any of this to happen.

Yussuf: I know. Now I fight.

Thelma: Is that the answer?

Yussuf: Only Allah knows the answers. But I fight.

Thelma: I hear things are going bad for you Yemenis.

Yussuf: I must be ready for the next fight.

Thelma: Why don't we go to the pictures? *Gold Diggers of Broadway* at the Grand Electric. One of them colour films.

Yussuf: I have no time. Sorry.

Thelma: Yussuf, I love you.

Yussuf: Yes, I know.

Thelma: Maybe that's my faith eh?

Yussuf: Your faith?

Thelma: You and Islam. Maybe my faith is love. Ours. There's no Book, no prophet, but — *(THEY EMBRACE).*

Sharp: Alright Yussuf. It's time *(WE GO INTO ANOTHER FIGHT. AGAIN YUSSUF DESTROYS HIS OPPONENT*

58

RUTHLESSLY) It's like the Devil's got into you Yussuf. The Maqbanah Mauler, eh? Who can beat him?

Yussuf: No-one can beat me *(GETS PRIZE MONEY)*.

Thelma: Yussuf I'm frightened.

Yussuf: Frightened.

Thelma: About you and me. What's happening?

Yussuf: I see the white men in the ring. And they cannot beat me. Me, the Arab the Yemeni. The inferior one. They are not good enough. Maybe your dad is right. Maybe we do not mix. Except in that ring.

Thelma: You mustn't believe that.

Yussuf: Why not? In the ring it is me who is left standing.

(NOW MAYBE STYLISE YUSSUF WINNING MORE: FIGHTS. FIGHTS HIS WAY OFF STAGE. ENTER CHARTERS WEARING A TOWEL READY FOR HIS MASSAGE).

Charters: Now where's that bloody masseuse? *(ENTER NEWS VENDOR HASTILY CHANGING HIS APPAREL).*

News vendor: Right here sir! *(CHARTERS LIES DOWN FOR HIS MASSAGE).*

Charters: Make sure you've taken the chill out of that massage oil lad.

News vendor: It's the temperature of virgin's blood sir!

Charters: I want a good massage but I don't want pummelling. The wife reckons I've got a bit of a spare tyre.

News vendor: You mean sir, your beloved is not in total raptures over your Adonis style figure?

Charters: *(LOOKS AT HIM CLOSELY)* Did you ever work as a waiter?

News vendor: Me sir? The very idea!

Charters: How about a barber?

News vendor: I wouldn't know a hair clipper from a lawn mower sir!

Charters: An undertaker?

News vendor: An undertaker!

Charters: Is that Ellis fellow around? *(ENTER ELLIS)*.

Ellis: I'm here.

Charters: Tell me the latest Ellis.

Ellis: The Arab seamen are boycotting the ships in South Shields.

Charters: And the white seamen?

Ellis: Mostly still signing on, despite pressure from the Minority Movement.

Charters: I see.

Ellis: They're calling a big meeting. For solidarity.

Charters: In my experience, solidarity counts for no more than a witch's tit if you've got an empty plate.

Ellis: The new rota system isn't going to help.

Charters: Your union agreed to bring it in. And it's worked in Antwerp.

Ellis: I'm just a bit worried Mr Charters. That it's a divisive measure.

Charters: The rota system applies to all seamen regardless of race or colour.

Ellis: Those longest ashore get preference for work. Which means the white seamen.

Charters: Are you telling me Ellis, that you are being openly critical of this new system, introduced with your full co-operation after long and frank discussions with the Federation?

Ellis: It's just that with time to think it over —

Charters: I need to know whether the Shipping Federation can, as in the past and with the overall improvement of this industry as the objective, rely on your co-operation and expert input. Basically Ellis, are we talking harmony here, or dissent?

Ellis: Well, I —

Charters: This is vitally important before we go any further.

Ellis: I can see big problems ahead.

Charters: Where do you stand man? On this rota system? Well?

Ellis: The National Union of Seamen will give full support to the rota system. In Hull, Cardiff and South Shields.

Charters: Good man Ellis. *(TO NEWS VENDOR)* Bloody hell — go steady lad! It's not some piece of putty you're pummelling!

News vendor: Your total comfort is my only ambition sir.

Charters: You give out more bullshit than a field full of charolais. Now don't look so troubled Ellis. People don't understand the kind of pressure we're under. Running vast fleets of ships when the world's economy is hanging by a thread.

Look at America. Falling apart. And everyone thinks they can turn up and be given jobs just like that wherever they come from. Like babies in a pram waiting for the next sweet.Well, too many sweets can be bad for babies. Oye! Are you a bloody psychopath? That's enough for me.*(GETS OFF SLAB AND WALKS OFF)*.

News vendor: *(DOING QUICK CHANGE)* Newspaper Mr Ellis?

Ellis: What?

News vendor: Just thought you might like to buy today's *Shields Gazette*. England all out for 421 against the Aussies. Fairfax takes four for 101. New Road Traffic Bill expected — 20 mph speed limit likely to be abolished. Read all about it. *(ELLIS BUYS NEWSPAPER)*. Nice weather for June eh?

Ellis: Yes *(EXITS)*.

(GEORGE IS READING THE PAPER. ENTER MARGARET).

Margaret: Say something to me George. Anything. I can't stand this silence. What do you want me to do? Maybe what I said was true, maybe it wasn't, but if you want me to say I'm sorry, I'll say it if that gets you to speak to me. There, I'm sorry. George.

(GEORGE GETS UP AND WALKS PAST HER TO GIVE ATTENTION TO HIS MODEL BOAT).

(YUSSUF IS FIGHTING, STYLISED TO SEE HIM WINNING EVERY BOUT. HE KNOCKS FINAL MAN DOWN. WHILE HE IS TRIUMPHANT AND IS BEING OBSERVED BY SHARP, THE PROMOTER HARRY ENTERS).

Harry: Alright, that's it Sharp.

Sharp: How do you mean?

Harry: I mean that Arab lad of yours, the Maqbana Mauler or whatever you call him.

Sharp: What about him?

Harry: No more fights.

Sharp: What's that supposed to mean?

Harry: What it says. A lot of tensions round in Shields at the moment with the Arabs. He's making it worse.

Sharp: You mean you don't mind the Arab street fighter, as long as he's losing.

Harry: This is the word on the street. They're coming here, taking our jobs. Now they're causing industrial unrest. And taking all the prize money in the blood pit.

Sharp: So?

Harry: So you'll get no more takers for your Arab lad.

(EXIT HARRY. SHARP GOES OVER TO YUSSUF. MIMES GIVING HIM THIS INFORMATION. YUSSUF'S SPARRING AND SHADOW BOXING SLOWLY SUBSIDE AS HE TAKES IT ON BOARD. EXIT SHARP. ENTER THELMA).

Thelma: There's more than one way of fighting Yussuf. *(PAUSE)* I know you have to prove yourself. Best way to prove yourself is to fight for others, not just yourself. That's what Allah would say. And Allah has the answer doesn't he? And I have the faith. In you. *(THEY EMBRACE).*

Trimdon: *(ENTERS TO MAKE A RALLY SPEECH)* Comrades, I have on the platform with me today Yussuf Abdullah Kuresh, known to many of you as the Maqbanah Mauler. They couldn't defeat him as a street fighter, and they won't defeat him with capitalism. Brother Yussuf, a few words from you.

Yussuf: We have nothing left to lose. We must stand firm. I came to this country for a new life. Soon Arabs in this country will have no life *(THELMA, GEORGE AND MARGARET OBSERVE THIS).*

Trimdon: Comrades, Yussuf speaks true. We have a common enemy. It is British capitalism and the Labour government. And just as you Arabs are being prosecuted here, so capitalism and this Labour government are sending gun boats even now against Arabs in Egypt, just as they have sent aircraft to bomb Arabs in Palestine. We call upon seamen of whatever nationality to assemble for a demonstration at Mill Dam. Join the Seamen's Minority Movement, join the Communist Party. Defeat the ship owners, the PC5 and the rota system. Black and white — unite and fight!

(ENTER CHARTERS STAGE SIDE WITH ELLIS IN TOW).

Charters: Do you think he gives a monkey's toss about those Arab seamen Ellis? He wants to bring down the government at any cost. If he thought it would stir up enough trouble, he'd be up there campaigning for monkeys to have two willies. Word from on high Ellis is that they want shut of these agitators. You sorted out a few good NUS men did you?

Ellis: They'll be ready if needed.

Charters: The way things are going, they will be needed. See those Arabs? Just looking for trouble. They've got knives, chair legs, paving stones. And that loud mouth Arab up there isn't helping. Make sure we get him.

Yussuf: I ask all my fellow Arab seamen to stand firm. Do not sign on.

Charters: If it's trouble they want, it's trouble they'll get. Police are ready.

Trimdon: Brother Yussuf has done brilliantly. The Arabs are 100 per cent! Not a single one of them has signed on and they are holding the picket line! Now it's up to you white sailors. Stand firm! South Shields must be the storm centre. All the other ports are looking to you as an example. Stand firm!

Charters: Make sure those seamen of yours break through the picket line at the signal Ellis.

Ellis: This is looking very ugly.

Charters: A man's got every right to sign on for work in his own country. Can't have that taken away. I want your men to break through the lines and get into the

Board of Trade offices.

Ellis: It'll erupt.

Charters: That's what happens to volcanoes. Right. Go.

(THE MEN BREAK THROUGH, TROUBLE ERUPTS AND THE RIOT ENSUES. YUSSUF IS PROMINENT AND MANAGES TO AVOID ARREST VIA HIS FIGHTING SKILLS. ONE STABBING. EXTENT OF RIOT CHOREOGRAPHY DEPENDS ON NUMBERS AND RESOURCES AVAILABLE).

Charters: Get that bloody Arab trouble-maker! *(FAIL TO GET YUSSUF. RIOT SUBSIDES. IN THE AFTERMATH NEWS VENDOR WALKS AMONG THE WRECKAGE).*

News vendor: Mass arrest at Mill Dam! Twenty-one Arabs and five members of the Seamen's Minority Movement taken in. One police officer stabbed. *(THELMA IS DESPERATLEY LOOKING FOR YUSSUF. EVENTUALLY FINDS HIM AND THEY EMBRACE).*

Thelma: Just hold me Yussuf.

Yussuf: It has gone very bad for us Thelma.

Thelma: At least you are free. What will happen to the others?

(MUSLIM MUSIC. ENTER YEMENI SEAMEN WHO TAKE UP PRAYER POSITIONS. AS THE FOLLOWING NAMES ARE READ OUT NEWS VENDOR MOVES AMONG THE MEN, TAPS THEM ON THE SHOULDER AND THEY LEAVE THE STAGE. HE READS FROM THE GAZETTE).

News vendor: Mr Ali Said, sentenced to 16 months hard labour and deportation. Ali Saleh, 12 months hard labour and deportation.

Yussuf: The Arab resistance is crushed. The Seamen's Minority Movement is no more.

News vendor: Thibuth Mohammed, six months hard

labour and deportation Mohammed Youssef, six months hard labour and deportation.

Thelma: And the boarding house?

Yussuf: The boarding house is closed Thelma. How can Mr Hassan afford to run it?

News vendor: Saleh Ahmed. Four months hard labour and deportation.
Abdul Ali. Eight months hard labour and deportation.

Thelma: I brought you some food.

Yussuf: Thank you *(WOLFS IT DOWN)* Allah will provide.

Thelma: Winter will soon be setting in. We must help you.

Naval officer: Abdul Mayal, 12 months hard labour. Abdul Mohammed, Four months hard labour and deportation.

Thelma: You have nothing. You must apply to the Public Assistance Committee for Outdoor Relief. This is a civilised country.

News vendor: Functionary — an application!

(NEWS VENDOR BRINGS ON FUNCTIONARY AND HIS DESK).

Functionary: *(STAMPING FORM)* Application denied.

News vendor: Ali Anon, eight months hard labour and deportation. Abdul Azzid, four months hard labour and deportation.

Thelma: Yussuf, what can we do?

Yussuf: The boarding house masters must appeal to the National Union *(ENTER ALI TO READ OUT LETTER TO UNION. FINAL PART OF LETTER IS READ ALOUD BY ELLIS AS HE ENTERS)*.

Ali: "Dear sirs, We see nothing but starvation ahead for we are like a lot of convicts with nothing to eat and all this through our union.. *(ENTER ELLIS)*.

Ellis: ...we all call on you and hope and pray to God that you will answer our appeal." I cannot be expected to deal with this. I am handing it over to the Colonial Office.

News vendor: Salem Kaleb, 12 months hard labour and deportation *(ENTER FOREIGN OFFICE OFFICIAL TO TAKE LETTER)*.

Foreign Office official: Take a letter Miss Prism *(WALKS ABOUT DICTATING)*. "I'm afraid the situation regarding the debt of the Arab seamen is a matter for the seamen themselves and their boarding house masters who I understand act on their behalf. To say that the Arab unemployment is down to the rota system is totally fallacious. Spell 'fallacious' can you Miss Prism? Good — Unemployment affects both British and Arab seamen and is due to the general depression." — two s's in depression of course. That will be all Miss Prism.

News vendor: Ibrahim Ahmed, 12 months hard labour and deportation.

Thelma: He can't live like this mam. No-one should have to.

Margaret: What can we do Thelma?

Thelma: You could ask dad to take him in.

Margaret: Take him in? Our house?

Thelma: He has no home. He has no money. He has nowhere to go.

Margaret: Your dad hasn't spoken a word to me since that day.

Thelma: Nor me. And look what it's doing to all of us.

67

Margaret: You're asking for miracles pet.

News vendor: Abdul Meage, four months hard labour and deportation.

Thelma: There has to be something we can do.

Charters: There is always something you can do.

Thelma: What do you mean?

Charters: That fancy Arab lad of yours — he can apply for indoor relief. At the Harton Institute.

Thelma: Why are you telling me this?

Charters: Him and his mates, they'll get a roof over their heads, food and bedding.

Thelma: The Harton Institute — the Shields Work house?

Charters: What's in a name? Good day.

News vendor: Abdul Mohammed, Four months hard labour and deportation. Said Sad, six months hard labour and deportation.

(ENTER YUSSUF TO OBSERVE THE LAST OF THE YEMENIS BE LED AWAY).

Mohammed Ahmed 15 months hard labour. Abdulla Saleh, 12 months hard labour and deportation.

Thelma: Yussuf, take this. It's the last few pounds I'm afraid.

Yussuf: I cannot take any more from you Thelma. This is not your fault.

Thelma: I love you Yussuf. What's mine is yours.

Yussuf: And what is mine is yours. Except nothing is mine.

Thelma: What about this Harton place?

Yussuf: In my country we say Allah will provide.

68

Thelma: I'm not sure they've given Allah a work permit in Shields, Yussuf. At least Harton might give you — something.

Yussuf: Yes. I will try.

(NEWS VENDOR SUMMONS FUNCTIONARY WITH HIS DESK WHO COMES ON FUSSILY).

Functionary: Very well, very well. Yussuf Abdullah Kuresh?

Yussuf: Yes.

Functionary: You wish to apply for indoor relief at the Harton Institute?

Yussuf: I do not wish to, but I shall.

Functionary: Kindly answer yes or no.

Yussuf: Yes.

Functionary: You agree to abide by the terms and conditions that apply to such an application?

Yussuf: I know nothing of such things.

Functionary: I do not wish to remind you again. You must answer yes or no.

Yussuf: Yes.

Functionary: Very well *(BIT OF FORM STAMPING ETC)* I wish to inform you that your application has been succesful. You are now allowed basic residence and sustenance at the Harton Institute. In the company, I might say, of a considerable number of your countrymen.

Yussuf: Thank you.

Thelma: It's better than nothing Yussuf — for the time being.

Functionary: You agreed to abide by the terms and conditions that apply to such an application. It is implicit within this permission that any alien applying for indoor relief within 12 months. of entering this country renders himself liable for deportation.

Yussuf: What?

Functionary: In the absence of any British citizenship, your status as an alien is taken as read.

News vendor: He came from Aden. Aden is British. That makes him British!

Charters: From Aden? The Maqbanah Mauler?

Functionary: It is my duty to inform you that a deportation order has now been issued against you.

Yussuf: What is happening? I don't understand —

Functionary: Arrangements will be made for your transportation out of South Shields and out of this country.

Thelma: But you can't do that — *(SETS ABOUT FUNCTIONARY)*.

Functionary: Kindly do not molest a local government officer. I bid you good day *(EXITS. ENTER PC)*.

PC: Step this way son. You'll be kept in the cells till you leave.

(YUSSUF BREAKS AWAY WHEN PC TRIES TO ARREST HIM. PURSUED BY PC SOUNDING WHISTLE. LATER WHOLE FAMILY VIEWS YUSSUF AS HE WANDERS ALONE & LONELY.).

Thelma: So you're just going to leave him out there like a hunted animal are you dad? The only man your daughter's ever loved? The only man who could ever make her happy? He's not your enemy dad. He's just like you, don't you see that? They dispose of the both of you when it suits their purposes. "Send the Arabs home!" Oh yes, you do their dirty work for them dad, why not? And what's it all doing to you and mam meantime? And what's it all doing to all of us? But you just keep going dad.You're doing just fine.

George: *(AFTER A PAUSE)* Let the lad in. *(YUSSUF ENTERS. MUM ENTERS.GEORGE STOPS HER)* I'll expect me tea the normal time.

(INTO CHARTERS AND ELLIS DRINKING IN ELLIS' PRIVATE CLUB. NEWS VENDOR IS THE BARMAN).

Charters: You're new to this club aren't you barman?

News vendor: Spanking new sir. As a pin.

Charters: How long have you been here exactly?

News vendor: About two minutes sir.

Charters: Give me a G & T and best make it a double. What will you have Ellis?

Ellis: I'd best stick to half a bitter.

Charters: Loyal to your working class roots, eh?

Ellis: Not quite sure what I'm doing in a club like this.

Charters: You don't get red leather like that in the Boilermakers Arms, eh? You look troubled Ellis.

Ellis: The situation's dire for the South Shields Arabs.

Charters: They came to this country for work. They went on strike, they caused violence and mayhem, I mean —

Ellis: Yes, I know, but —

News vendor: If I could just be so bold as to say something Mr Ellis, sir?

Ellis: What?

News vendor: None of my business I know, and I'm

71

probably talking out of turn, but —

Ellis: Well, what did you want to say? Get on with it!

News vendor: It's just that — well, Mr Charters here. He despises you.

Ellis: What?

Charters: Always has done. He hasn't got even the most teen-weeny thimbleful of respect for you.

Ellis: What is all this?

Charters: The barman's smarter than he looks. Not saying much, mind.

Ellis: What's going on here Mr Charters?

Charters: Nothing much. Except you're a bloody disgrace to your union and always have been. No wonder they chucked you lot out the TUC.

Ellis: But I've always tried to co-operate with the Shipping Federation and —

Charters: It's not your job to co-operate with us son. It's your job to squeeze us as hard as you can for your members. Just like we squeeze you.

Ellis: You know I've never believed in confrontation!

Charters: What you doing in this job then? This is business son. It's about making profit. We make as much as we can. You try to stop us. Simple really. And you know what? I quite like the arrangement.

Ellis: But all the help and support I've given the Federation!

Charters: He still doesn't get it, does he barman?

News vendor: He seems slightly short of the rudiment-aries, I must admit.

Charters: You've been a disaster for your members, do

you know that Ellis? You've allowed me to be as big a bastard as I like, and believe me, I can be one hell of a bastard. You've allowed me to stitch you up 100 per cent. And you just rolled over like some soppy dog. It's all been a bit — well, dull really.

News vendor: How about another half of bitter sir — on the house?

Charters: Why not have one yourself barman, on me?

Naval officer: Why not go screw yourself?

Charters: Fair comment. Well goodbye Ellis, I have a feeling we won't meet again. That's me about done *(EXIT CHARTERS)*.

News vendor: That's you about done too sir, if I'm not much mistaken *(EXIT ELLIS)*.

(THE CHARLTON HOUSEHOLD. GEORGE IS BUSY WITH HIS BOAT. YUSSUF IS WATCHING).

Yussuf: You would like me to help you Mr Charlton?

George: No need lad. Can do it best myself.

Yussuf: Yes.

George: That street fighting — come natural to you does it?

Yussuf: Back home in Maqbanah, often we fought. Just for fun.

George: And you always won?

Yussuf: Every time.

George: Best watch myself then, eh?

Yussuf: Yes, or I will — how do you say — sweep the carpet with you?

George: Wipe the floor.

Yussuf: OK. I was going to make in big in England.

George: Aye well. Fireman were you?

Yussuf: Only one sailing.

George: Mucky job fireman. I was an able-bodied seaman. Not any more. Still, that's not your problem *(ENTER MARGARET)*.

Margaret: They were selling off meat pies cheap at Dewhursts. I got six. Are you alright Yussuf?

Yussuf: Give me something to do.

Margaret: You could peel some spuds. Look out for the black bits.

George: Margaret!

Margaret: Sorry, I didn't mean —

Yussuf: Mr Charlton, Mrs Charlton, it is very good of you to shelter me, but I feel —

George: Feel what son?

Yussuf: I don't know what I feel.

Margaret: It might all blow over soon eh? They'll forget all about you and then — well.

Yussuf: I have brought trouble to this house.

George: Now don't talk bloody daft.

Yussuf: I have brought trouble to Thelma.

Margaret: You love her son.

Yussuf: Of course. More than anything.

Margaret: Well then *(KNOCK AT DOOR)* Who's that?

George: I'll get it *(GOES TO DOOR. IT IS A PC)*.

PC: Sorry to disturb you George. I believe you have living on these premises a certain Yussuf Abdullah Kuresh.

George: What?

PC: The aforesaid Mr Kuresh is in fact an illegal immigrant and a deportation order has been served upon him. I must ask you to hand him over to the authorities.

George: And what if I tell you I've no idea what you're talking about?

PC: Then I have to tell you that obstructing the law is a chargeable offence. As is illegally harbouring an alien.

George: Look, I'm just about to have me dinner, so why don't you clear off?

PC: Come along now George, don't make it hard for yourself.

Yussuf: *(COMES FORWARD INTO DOORWAY)* No, don't make it hard for yourself.

PC: Yussuf Abdullah Kuresh? I must ask you to accompany me to the station.I'm afraid I have to apply these *(PUTS ON HANDCUFFS)*.

Yussuf: A man cannot live like a hunted dog. Thank you. You are good people.

Margaret: But they can't just take you like that and —

George: Bastards.

PC: Sorry about this George. Just doing my job.

Margaret: But where will they send him and —

PC: *(TAKING YUSSUF AWAY)* Just doing my job *(THEY EXIT. A FEW SECONDS LATER THELMA RUNS ON)*.

Thelma: Yussuf! I met this man today and he says he can give you a bit of work on the side till things calm down and — *(SHE TAKES IN THE SCENE)* Yussuf? Yussuf!

(ENTER NEWS VENDOR READING FROM THE GAZETTE).

News vendor: The men who went last night had not committed any crime. Just before 9.30 the thirty-eight men came from the cells at the Central Police Station past a double line of police officers into the two waiting police patrol cars. They were driven to the goods entrance of the railway station and lined up at the end of the platform. They were very quiet. At 9.50 the train steamed out of the station and bore the Arabs away from South Shields.

END OF PLAY

Cast List for the
2008 Performances

Yussuf
A young Yemeni seaman   Amir Boutrous

Thelma
A South Shields lass   Janine Leigh-Allen

George
Thelma's dad   Neil Armstrong

Margaret
Thelma's mother   Ann Ridley

News vendor
The play's everyman   Charlie Richmond

Charters
A shipping fed. exec.   Jim Kitson

Ellis
NUS secretary   Paul Court

Ali Hassan
Boarding house keeper   Neji Neja

Naval officer *et al.*
Various parts   Harry Gallagher

Fight Manager *et al.*
Various parts   Iain Cunningham

Supporting cast
Fight scenes, boarding   Raeef Abdulla
house, political meetings,   Sean Ferguson
riot scene   Danny Kendal
          Michael Lockhart
          Anthony Miller
          Peter Murray
          Stacey Rayer

The play takes place in South Shields, 1929-30, and briefly off the coast of Yemen in the first half of the 19th century.

الشَّغَب

ساوث شيلدز 1930

مسرحية للكاتب البريطاني
بيتر مورتيمر

ترجمة:
عبدالعالم الشميري

Five Leaves Publications
www.fiveleaves.co.uk

بسم الله الرحمن الرحيم

عُرضت هذه المسرحية لأول مرة، على مسرح "كستمز هاوس"، في مدينة ساوث شيلدز البريطانية، خلال الفترة من يوم الاثنين الموافق 24 أكتوبر، إلى يوم الجمعة الموافق 28 أكتوبر 2005. وسيتم عرضها ثانية على المسرح نفسه، كما سيتم عرضها على مسرح "يُنيتي" في مدينة ليفربول البريطانية خلال صيف 2008.

Riot

was published in 2008 by
Five Leaves Publications,
PO Box 8786, Nottingham NG1 9AW
www.fiveleaves.co.uk
info@fiveleaves.co.uk

English Cover images: Cloud Nine/ARTS UK
Arabic Cover design: Waleed Fikri
ISBN: 978 1 905512 49 2
Five Leaves acknowledges financial support from Arts Council
England

Five Leaves is a member of Inpress
(www.inpressbooks.co.uk),
representing independent publishers

Typeset and designed by Four Sheets Design and Print
Printed in Great Britain

بسم الله الرحمن الرحيم

مقدمة المترجم

المتصفح في أوراق التاريخ، يجد أن الجالية اليمنية المتواجدة في المملكة المتحدة يعود تاريخها إلى ما قبل العام 1885م، عندما غادر كثير من أبناء اليمن بلادهم بحثًا عن العمل وكسب العيش فاستقر معظمهم ـ ممن عمل على متن السفن التجارية البريطانية ـ في الموانئ البريطانية مثل (ساوث شيلدز ـ كارديف ـ هل ـ وليفربول) .

وعندما نشبت الحرب العالمية الأولى، واتجه البريطانيون صوب أرض المعركة، كانت الحاجة تتطلب البحث عن عمّال على متن السفن التجارية عوضًا عن العمال البريطانيين الذين غادروا أعمالهم باتجاه المعركة، فلم يجد أرباب السفن سوى اليمنيين المتواجدين هناك ممن لم يشارك في خوض المعارك مع إخوانهم البريطانيين.

لقد اشتهر اليمنيون بإخلاصهم وتفانيهم في العمل مما زاد تمسك أرباب السفن بهم، غير أن ذلك لم يتوافق مع كثير من البحارة البريطانيين الذين عادوا من الحرب فوجدوا اليمنيين قد احتلوا أماكنهم في العمل، الأمر الذي أجج الغيرة في نفوسهم، ودعا داعي العنصرية في أوساطهم، فعملوا على الضغط على اتحاد الشحن تارة، والهيئات النقابية تارة أخرى، مطالبين إياهم استصدار قرار أو قانون يمنع اليمنيين من العمل على ظهور السفن. وبعد استصدار ذلك القرار بدأت الحياة تتعكر في أوساط الجالية اليمنية؛ فأخذوا يطالبون بإلغاء هذا القرار دون جدوى، فبدأ الإضراب، ثم المسيرات السلمية، والتي واجهتها السلطات البريطانية بالقمع، الأمر الذي أدى إلى حدوث الشغب الذي استلهم منه الكاتب (بيتر موريتمر) هذه المسرحية التي تؤرخ وجود اليمنيين في المملكة المتحدة.

ويعد الكاتب (بيتر موريتمر) من الكتاب البريطانيين المهتمين بأبناء الجالية اليمنية، ولقد كانت أول معرفتي به عندما قرأت في جريدة (شيلدز جازيت) خبرًا عن إصدار كتاب (Cool for Qat) للكاتب (بيتر مرتيمر) فبدأت البحث عنه، وعندما وجدته وعرف أني من اليمن تهلل وجهه ورحب بي كثيرا، وبدأ يسألني عن اليمن وأخبارها، عندها عرفت مدى الحب الذي يكنه هذا الرجل لأبناء الجالية اليمنية، وعرفت منه أنه قام بتأليف مسرحية (الشغب) التي تحكي معاناة الشاب اليمني (يوسف) بطل المسرحية الذي خرج من مدينته (مقبنة) بحثًا عن العمل في بريطانيا، وزاد تعلقه بي عندما عرف أنني من نفس مدينة البطل (يوسف). عندها طلب مني ترجمة المسرحية إلى العربية، فرحبت بذلك أيما ترحيب.

وهأنذا أقدمها لقراء العربية وقراء اليمن على وجه الخصوص ليعرفوا مدى المعاناة التي عاناها أبناؤهم ممن وصلوا إلى بلد الضباب.

عبدالعالم الشميري
هيلزوين، مايو 2008

4

مقدمة المؤلف

الكاتب المسرحي ليس مؤرخاً، ولا عالم اجتماع. وإنما كتابة المسرحية رحلة إلى المجهول – إلى وجهة غير معلومة.

عندما طلب مني مدير مسرح "كستمز هاوس" الثقافي السيد "راي سبنسر"، كتابة مسرحية تدور أحداثها حول أعمال الشغب التي دارت بين البحارة اليمنيين ونظرائهم البريطانيين في ساوث شيلدز يوم 2 أغسطس 1930، رفضت في بادئ الأمر لأنني لم أكن متأكدا من أي الأحداث أبداً. ومع أنني قد قبلت بعد ذلك، إلا أنني كنت لا أزال مترددا. وبعد ذلك أمضيت فترة من الوقت في التفكير. حيث طلب مني من الناس عدم خلط الأمور. فمع اضطراب العرقي في البلد - لاسيما بعد أحداث الحادي عشر من سبتمبر - كان عليّ أن أنسى موضوع هذه المسرحية، وأن أدع الفتنة نائمة، حيث كنا ننتظر مواجهة مباشرة بين الغرب والمسلمين. وقد استحوذ هذا الرأي على تفكيري أو كاد.

ولكنني قررت في نهاية الأمر السفر إلى اليمن وأقنعت المسؤولين في مجلس إنجلترا للفنون – فرع منطقة الشمال الشرقي لإنجلترا- بإعطائي منحة السفر. وقد كانت نصيحة المسؤولين الحكوميين هي عدم السفر إلى هذا البلد الخطير – حسب زعمهم- الذي يمكن أن يكون ملجأ لتنظيم القاعدة، كان ذلك مثل العديد من النصائح الحكومية، كان ذلك مجرد هراء. لم أكن أعلم ما الذي أبحث عنه، وعندما رجعت، لم أعرف ما إذا كنت قد وجدت ما أريد. لقد تركت هذه الرحلة آثاراً عميقة في نفسي حتى إنني كتبت كتاباً عنها أسميته – إستعدادا للقات، رحلة يمنية- (Cool for Qat – A Yemeni Journey)، كما أني كتبت هذه المسرحية أيضاً.

وخلال عامين من القراءة والسفر وإجراء الإتصالات الشخصية، والتصوير، قمت بإضافة أجزاء للصورة اليمنية. فلقد كنت أتناول حقبة من التاريخ كادت أن تنسى في بريطانيا، وكادت أن تنسى في اليمن أيضا. ومع أن هذه الحقبة كانت تحمل الكثير من الأمور المخزية إلا أنها أعطت درسا قاسيا لمدينة ساوث شيلدز، أعتقد أنها لن تنساه.

ربما تكون ساوث شيلدز من بين أقل الأماكن عنصرية في المملكة المتحدة في دنيا الناس الآن، وأعتقد أن تلك الحادثة التي وقعت في 2 أغسطس 1930، كان لها أثر امتد حتى أواننا هذا. وبالإضافة إلى ذلك، فإنني تستهويني المسرحيات التاريخية التي لها علاقة بواقعنا الحاضر، ويظل لأحداثها صدى يقرع آذاننا عبر امتداد السنين.

ومنذ العرض الأول للمسرحية في أكتوبر 2005، استفاد منها الكثيرون من سكان ساوث شيلدز اليمنيين، وحازت على شهرة كبيرة. حيث أن المسلسل الشهير "coast" الذي يعرض على BBC، قد تناول جزء من أحداث الشغب، كما أن معرض "آخر رجال القاموس" الذي أقيم في مركز "بولتيك" في شهر إبريل من العام الحالي قد لخص حياة اليمنيين في ساوث شيلدز وتاريخهم وقد لاقى إنتشارا واسعا.

وقد رفعت من شأن كل شخصية، على الرغم من أن كلا منها له أصل في واقع الحياة آنذاك. وتنحو المسرحية منحى سياسيا ولكنه في الوقت ذاته منحى شخصي يتضمن قصة حب، لأن كاتبي المسرحيات في غالب الأحيان يتناولون الموضوعات الكبيرة أولا ثم يتطرقون إلى الشخصيات وكيف يجب أن تكون. ومن مهام الكاتب أن ينير

5

بفكره ظلام هذا العالم. ولا شك أن هذه التجربة اليمنية قد أضاءت الطريق لي، وإذا نجحت أنا في أن أنقل إليك بعضاً من هذا الضياء، فقد قمت إذاً بواجبي.

لقد عرضت المسرحية أول ما عرضت في أكتوبر سنة 2005، كما أعيد عرضها في عام 2008 في "كستمز هاوس" ومن إنتاج "كلاود ناين". كما ستعرضت أيضاً في مهرجان ليفربول للفنون العربية كجزء من الاحتفالات الثقافية في ليفربول كعاصمة للثقافة الأوروبية للعام 2008. والمسرحية من إخراج السيد "دارين بالمر" وهو ينتمي إلى الجيل الثالث من اليمنيين في ساوث شيلدز، والذي كان جده يعمل مع حركة البحارة الأقلية وقت المظاهرات.

وقد استخدمنا اقتباسات مباشرة من جريدة "شيلدز جازيت" وكذلك مجلة "ذا سيمان" وهي المجلة الخاصة بالاتحاد الوطني للبحارة، حيث تناولت خطابات لأعضاء من حركة البحارة الأقلية، واقتبسنا كذلك من خطابات كتبها البحارة اليمنيون يطالبون فيها مساعدات مالية وأجاب عليها المسؤولون.

ولمعرفة المزيد من تاريخ الجالية اليمنية في "ساوث تاينسايد"، فإنني أوصي بقراءة كتاب من "تعز إلي تاينسايد" From Ta'izz to Tyneside للكاتب ريتشارد لوليس (مطابع جامعة إكستر 1995). إن حدث وحضرت هذه المسرحية في "كستمز هاوس" في مدينة "ساوث شيلدز" ودخلت من الباب الرئيسي للمسرح فمن المؤكد أنك ستشعر بالذهاب في رحلة عبر التاريخ لتقف عند ميدان "ميل دام" وتشهد الأحداث رأي العين.

بيتر مورتيمر
كالوركوتس، مايو 2008

6

قائمة الممثلين
(حسب ترتيب الظهور على خشبة المسرح)

يوسف	بحار يمني شاب
شارب*	مدير مباريات ملاكمة
هاري *	متعهد مباريات ملاكمة
بائع الصحف	بائع صحف/محترف تدليك/حلاق/نادل، والشخص العادي في المسرحية
عابر سبيل*	عابر سبيل
جورج تشارلتون	بحار سابق في ساوث شيلدز
ثيلما	ابنة جورج تشارلتون
مارجريت	زوجة جورج تشارلتون
تشارترز	موظف تنفيذي في اتحاد الشحن
إليس	سكرتير الاتحاد الوطني للبحارة
علي حسن	مدير نُزل للبحارة في ساوث شيلدز
الموظف*	موظف إداري
الشاب *	شاب سكران من جيبوردي
البحاران*	بحاران على متن سفينة في ساوث شيلدز
الضابط البحري*	ضابط بحري بريطاني في القرن التاسع عشر
الشريف*	تاجر شحن من القرن التاسع عشر
تريمدون*	ناشط سياسي، وعضو في حركة البحارة الأقلية
المسؤول*	مسؤول مكتب الهجرة
الشرطي*	ضابط شرطة
إضافات	إضافات مختلفة لمشهد الشغب، ومشاهد الملاكمة، ومشاهد الخطب السياسية

الأجزاء التي وضعت عليها علامة " * " يمكن أداؤها بواسطة ممثلين اثنين معاً.

الفصل الأول

تقع أحداث المسرحية في ساوث شيلدز بين عامي 1929 و1930، وفي جزء موجز منها، في خليج عدن، خلال القرن التاسع عشر.

(يدخل يوسف، وهو يتظاهر بالملاكمة بطريقة قوية. يدخل شارب إلى جانب المسرح، ويدخل هاري إلى الجانب الآخر).

شارب	أفضل ملاكم شوارع شهدناه في شيلدز لعدة سنوات.
هاري	عربي قوي لعين، وملاكم شوارع؟
شارب	إنه يتمتع بتناغم حركي.
هاري	نعم، وهو يستمر في حصد الجوائز، يا شارب.
شارب	هذا ما يفعله الفائزون، فهم يفوزون بالمال. ولهذا، فإنني أحب إدارة أعمالهم.
هاري	ربما يرسل بالمال كله إلى عدن اللعينة أو حيثما كان يعيش.
شارب	ماذا دهاك يا هاري، أليس لديك منافس لفتاي؟

(يدخل بائع صحف يبيع الجرائد)

بائع الصحف	عدد خاص! عدد خاص! اقرأ كل شيء! حملات السيد "شاتر إيد"؛ عضو ساوث شيلدز في البرلمان؛ لبناء جسر جديد فوق نهر التاين!، افتتاح متجر بنز الجديد في شارع الملك! عدد خاص! عدد خاص! *(يلاحظ بائع الصحف وجود آخرين).* أنتما الاثنان، ابتعدا عن المسرح، إنكما تستبقان الأحداث قليلا هنا فالقصة لم تبدأ بعد. فالفتى المسكين قد وصل للتو إلى شيلدز *(يخرج شارب وهاري)*. *(يساعد يوسف على ارتداء ملابسه اليمنية التقليدية)*. تفضل. نحن الآن في ساوث شيلدز عام 1929، وقد ابتعد هذا الفتى كثيرا عن وطنه. إن ساوث شيلدز مدينة صعبة. فالشرطة تفتش كل حانة، بحثا عن مباراة في الملاكمة، مساء يوم السبت. وإذا لم تكن هناك مباراة، فإنهم يفتعلون مباراة. حسنا يا بني! من الأفضل لك أن تبحث عن الطريق التي تقودك إلى المكان الذي تريد. حظًا سعيدا.

(يخرج بائع الصحف. وفي النهاية، يوقف يوسف عابر سبيل).

يوسف	من فضلك؟
عابر السبيل	ماذا أيها الفتى النحيف؟
يوسف	أريد أن أجد –
عابر السبيل	ارفع صوتك، فإنني لا أكاد أسمعك.

(يخرج يوسف قطعة من الورق، ويقرأها عابر السبيل).

8

أنت تريد أن تذهب إلى "وست هولبرن"، أليس كذلك؟ حسنًا يبدو لي أنه كذلك. إنها في هذا الاتجاه يا رجل. بعد "مل دام" واستمر في السير بمحاذاة النهر. وسوف تجد "وست هولبرن". إنه أشبه بعض الشيء بمكان قذر.

يوسف	السيد/ علي حسن.
عابر السبيل	ما هذا؟
يوسف	إنني أبحث عن السيد/ علي حسن.
عابر السبيل	إنني لا أعرف أحدًا بهذا الاسم. كيف لي أن أعرف، أليس كذلك؟ من أين أنت إذًا؟
يوسف	عفوًا؟
عابر السبيل	حسنًا، لا داعي للاعتذار يا بني. من أين أنت؟
يوسف	إنني من اليمن.
عابر السبيل	آه، اليمن؟ لا شك أن الطقس شديد الحرارة في اليمن. هناك الكثير من اليمنيين في شيلدز الآن. العديد منهم، حسبما يقول البعض.
يوسف	آسف، إنني –
عابر السبيل	ليس أنا بالطبع. عش ودع الآخرين يعيشون، فهذا ما أقوله. طالما أن كل فرد يعلم مكانه. هل أنت بخير الآن يا بني؟
يوسف	بخير؟
عابر السبيل	سر فقط بمحاذاة النهر. إنه نهر "التاين" يا بني. أحد أشهر الأنهار في العالم. لا شك أنه ليس لديكم نهر مثله في اليمن.
يوسف	لا، أنا –
عابر السبيل	ابق قريبًا من النهر يا بني، وسوف تكون في "وست هولبرن" قبل أن تدرك ذلك.

(يخرج الاثنان. تعزف موسيقى إسلامية. يبدو أن هناك صوت أذان للصلاة. يختفي الصوت فجأة ويظهر صوت أوركسترا جاك هيلتون. تدخل ثيلما وهي ترقص ممسكة بوسادة. ترقص لبرهة. يدخل الوالد؛ جورج تشارلتون، حيث يسير متعرجًا، ثم يغلق صوت الموسيقى).

ثيلما	أبي!
جورج	صوت مزعج لعين.
ثيلما	إنها أوركسترا "جاك هيلتون" يا أبي!
جورج	لقد سمعت أصواتًا مزعجة، أفضل من هذا بكثير.

(تدخل الأم مارجريت)

مارجريت	دع ثيلما تسمع موسيقاها يا جورج.
جورج	هل تسمين هذه موسيقى؟

9

ثيلما	إنها الموسيقى الأكثر شعبية في صالات الرقص.
جورج	على أية حال، لماذا تتزين هكذا؟
مارجريت	ثيلما ذاهبة إلى الخارج، أليس كذلك يا ثيلما؟
ثيلما	إنني ذاهبة للرقص.
جورج	الرقص؟
ثيلما	وهل تتوقع مني البقاء في البيت كل ليلة؟!
جورج	يمكنك البقاء في البيت ومساعدة والدتك.
مارجريت	لا عليك يا جورج، إنني لا أحتاج أي مساعدة.
جورج	هل أحضرت الخمر الخاصة بي؟ *(تفتح مارجريت زجاجةً له).*
مارجريت	لقد أحضرت لك ثلاث زجاجات. سعرها جنيه وثلاثة بنسات.
جورج	لا تقلقي، سوف أشرب بأبطأ ما أستطيع.
مارجريت	إنني لم أقصد، أنا –
جورج	إنها سعادة الرجل في الحياة *(يشرب)* حتى إذا لم يكن يستطيع شراءها بنفسه. على أية حال، لا يجب عليها الخروج طوال الوقت هكذا.
ثيلما	إنني أريد بعض الإثارة. وليس هناك الكثير من ذلك في شيلدز *(ترقص مرة أخرى وبيدها الوسادة)*
جورج	إنك تريدين معرفة شاب، أليس كذلك؟
مارجريت	هل هذا صحيح يا ثيلما؟ هل ترغبين في ذلك؟
ثيلما	هل رأيتم معظم الشباب في حيّنا؟
	(يدخل بائع الصحف، ويبدأ في الرقص معها)
بائع الصحف	شاب يجذبك إليه، أليس كذلك؟
ثيلما	آه، نعم!
بائع الصحف	غريب أسمر البشرة، مليء بالعاطفة والغموض.
ثيلما	إن لك طريقة في اختيار الكلمات يا بائع الصحف.
	(يواصل بائع الصحف عمله)
بائع الصحف	الطبعة الأخيرة! عدد خاص! "جراف زيبيلين" يصل إلى أمريكا! 100.000 يحيّون المنطاد في "نيو جيرزي"! اقرأ هذه الأخبار! *(يبيع نسخة للوالد)*
جورج	لقد عرفت الإثارة ذات مرة.
بائع الصحف	حقاً؟
جورج	لقد جبت نصف العالم ورجعت. سافرت في سفن كبيرة وسفن صغيرة وفي الأسطول التجاري والأسطول الملكي. لقد اكتسبت خبرة كبيرة من ذلك. والسفينة الوحيدة التي أمتلكها الآن هي هذه. *(يشير إلى نموذج سفينة يقوم ببنائه).*

10

بائع الصحف *(يخرج. الصفحة الرابعة. الكلمات المتقاطعة.* ويبقى جورج على مسرح يقرأ إلى قاربه. بائع الصحف يرحم رض المشهد التالي للمستمع " تشاترتز والبيس" حيث يقلي تشاترتز كلمة.)

تشاترتز | تحرك يا بني. هل إلى أي دفعة لك تتحرك؟

بائع الصحف | آسف يا سيدي. ها أنا اذ.

تشاترتز | أريد أيها السادة السيديات ينبئ، حدث أختم أن السادة لؤسؤكمسكن ينفذي عن اذننا. بلد في فة الحالية الاقتصادية الكواث اغفال عن تست فإنبان نحن،الشدان اتحاد بلد الإضرار بار رار نوون نوون بسبب اناتانتا معدم عدديدة تاو سنوات مر فة كله هذا ان بلدا في نتبع لكي الوقت حان فقد الأمر، دام وما مام،العا اتحاد في الآن في ريدون تقدم عن من عن أربع مكم أن وأريد التفشة اسة سيا كرأش لذلك،فإنبانا تتضحنات التقدم نقدن جميعا عليا ان أعضائه، من لعمل اسأ عن عن وواحد جنبيه هذه طاعاتها باسئة للبحارة الولوتنظ يقدم الذي عوبة أسا البيس له كل سيد شكرا البيس السا سيد.

(يظهر التقدير لالبيس). وشكركوا لكم جميعاً اسما ااحوا لي الآن، لأنني مشغول وقوله ادا

(تصفيق. يخرج تشاترتز ويتحدث إلى بائع الصحف. الداذل أيها؟

بائع الصحف | من؟ أنا؟

تشاترتز | قم بفرش هذه المنضدة، وأحضر رض بعض الطعاام.

(يدبر) بائع الصحف ملاسم الناداذ، ويحضر منضدة ااعدة عليها بعض الطعاام. الفاخر. وزجاجة من الخمر. ثم يتقدم البيس)

البيس | خاطب رائع يا سيد تشاترتز.

تشاترتز | أعلم ما يجب علي فعله يا البيس أيها الناداذ! إنني أشم رائحة الفلين *(يشرب)* في هذه الخمر. يجب عليك أن تعرف أن هذه الخمر، لذا يجب أن يكون شيئا أفضل حظك أنني أن أدفع ثمن هذه الخمر. هذا. من فضل من نسح من. مالي من

| هل يمكن أن أقدم لك كون "شاتوثونينيون" صص عنع الذا، باب يد كل 1925 يا سيدي؟

تشاترتز | أنت لا تستطيع أن تعرف الخمر الجيدة من القيء،فأغلق كم العينين. اطلب من الناداذ الملم أن يحضر لي خمرا جديدة، وإلا واجه العواقب.

| معن سيدي. إن طيب يدي سيدي. ادا *(يخرج من المسرح).*

تشاترتز | والآن يا "البيس"، أريد أن أسر ّرّ بشيء إنه لك العربة.

البيس | العرب، سيد تشاترتز؟

تشاترتز | معن. منهم مهم. منكبة كانها معم. شيلد، واسواثوبولوبريفريفيفيد في داكراب من ديديد هم. الاتحاد الخاص بك أيضا. الأخرى ى أنهاموائ كانها من ديديد

البيس | إن الاتحاد الوطني يفتوح مفمة ارحبحلل لكل جنسيايات.

تشاترتز | معم. هل له أيها المااكار البيس عن ذلك كلك سمعت؟

البيس | معم،أعتقد ذلك.

تشاترتز | لمعيل ءلاوه العرب نينين للممسؤولونوليودمومن الرلا الشا مقدمدينيلرزل في ذلك للعيل العرب يأتون الذين ءلاوه هذ ولكل لأمر مثير للشفقة. إنه السفل. على نفن نوتون

11

نيينايطيرب اووسيلي ءلاؤه أن كش لا نِونيانطيرب أنهم نوموعزي زعدن من
أبسة ،ملكة لثل مِملثمف تهمِملتكة

(يدخل بانع الصحف)

بانع الصحف	في الواقع، إنها جاءت من هناكِ.
تشارترز	نعم، ماذا؟
بانع الصحف	ملكة أبس – جاءت من اليمِين.
تشارترز	أين هذه المخرأ أيها السيفية أرمز الخلا هذه الصغيرغير؟
بانع الصحف	هاي يا سيدي، *(ريص بكوبا. تنتهَقوفهقشتترزرز).*
تشارترز	كهناك فوف سِذلكَ *(بعد ذلك كُل يكأل فوس شسراهمَهاة،* والأمر يا سيلإلا أن هناكِ س فوف رمي رمر كناكِ، اذا انتقتنا في وقوعى في هذا البلد في أناسِ الطيبيين من ديدِ العرف هل تعرفِ. اذا؟ لمِاذا؟
إلليس	إننا رمر تمر تأوأبأت عصبِيةِ. التضمخر في ف الولايات المتحدةِ الأمِريكية، وخسارةِ لولِ ترترتيِ.
تشارترز	إن المزيد والمزيدِ ديدِ من الأفرار داراروبيحيي نون من قلبِ ليلِ جائفنَ. وخذ من عدد عن نهناكِ لذلكِ مثلا اتتناصِ صناعتَ أن بأن البعضِ وبقولِ العاملةَ. الأيديِ في فضانه هناكِ عليها. لا يصححوا يِ والوظافنَ، الذين يتستيتوحقوصولِ الحصولِ على ي
إلليس	أنا لست تأكداتمتسِ تترز يا كملكم كلامِ أفهمِ أنني من تأكداتمتسِ لست أنا
تشارترز	لقع. اذا كان ديدكِ ايها الندالِ، ه وبرأخر
بانع الصحف	هيه يبرش يذذِ الوقتِ في أنه هو قوله هو السيديواحي ما أعتقدُ اذا نائفنَ على حصل برواِ قد العرف من ديدِ نإن فإن الخمرِ من حجاجةِ الزِ هذه ف في هذا البلدِ.
تشر	أنت ثراكاةِ ،ثةِ تنكذكلكِ يلسِ اذا عندك من كذلكِ ؟ىوحلو
بانع الصحف	المصنوعونوعةِ التقاف ائرِ جديدةِ، وتورتةِ واستر، بيببِ زالبِ رائر فطانيِ ديانيِ لدل كريم في الطاز جواالآ سيسِ والكركِمِ في البيتِ، مريم.
تشارترز	ءيش لولاوانت تتنِ أستطيعِ أنني أعتقدُ لا. جائعِ لست لسنبأنِ أشعر الحقيقةِ، في آخرِ.
بانع الصحف	هيا يا سيديِ،ي، أن تأكلِ كنمكِ نائنًا آخر!
تشارترز	نكون ما نكيلِوي، ببيبِ بالزِ آخذ فطيرةِ زذ سوفِ حسنِ اننسِ. نعم
بانع الصحف	أرأيت تيت سيديِ؟ محقاقِ تنكت دقلِ تا يِ السيلِ
تشارترز	ظل في لِ؟ الراي رأيِ يقلي على السيلإلا يا تلءاسِ ه هل الللي،ببيانايا برريطيبانايا امام العالمِ في من هذه الأزمِ تِالتي رمر نمِ الاقتصاديةَ ؟هاتبِ
إلليس	رمِ الأمِ في ما أهم أهذا هو ،راجاحارِ للبببِ الوطونيِ نطليِ الاتحادِ لو نكمِيكنِ، اننا ،حسمِ
تشارترز	امدعن ما تحرمِ نكنِ ولكنِ. هيئنينِ من ههبِشيشبِم ما أو نحنحِ الشتاحِ اتحاداتِ لولِ يكمِنِ ولا هذا من فِ خطأفِ أن يعيِ ريرِ ديدِ فإبإنهِ، كافيةِ وجبةِ مِ الجِ رجلِ؟!اذا
بانع الصحف	ه كتِبجوبكِ تترزِ ديدِ سا يا تستمتعِ لِ
تشارترز	لقدِ تناولتِ أفضلِ منها. فكرِ فكرِ في الأمِ يا السيلإلا.
بانع الصحف	له من شِءيِ آخرِ يا سيديِ؟
تشارترز	أعتقدُ أننا قد اكتفينانيمنكِ.

12

فسوف يدخل إلى مكان آخر. في ةدضنملا فيظنتب ةلآلا نع باب ةصحصلا موقي)
اذه. نيلماعلل عباتلا لزنلا يف ,نسح يلع ىلإ. لامعلابلاقتيب. فوسوي جفترييو وسوي
.ةيبرعلا ةغللاب نوكي نأ بجي دهشملا)

يلع	انه. رارب شيء لكل ارتلجنإ هذه رعشت كنك)يئومسم فوسوي) يلبلاب درد كن انه. رارب درد نويناطيربلا فاد. نجس نويناطيربلا فد. مدملاو .طقسلا
فسوو	.نآلا يناطيرب انأ
يلع	تلبعح هل. نودقتعي لا مهنإ نويناطيربلا ةبرش يناي ءاوس نوكت نأ نكمي ينايطيربلا ةبرش نأ نودقتعي لا مهنإ اذا هذه موي يف لك نلبعن اننا)ايفا هساراس فوسوي زنيهز) ؟فوسو اي ايلا تسيل تلايارلا)ةيزيلجنإلابال) مالأ يأ لدل هل. النزل انه انا هذه ىلإ انثا)ةيزيلجنإل فوسوي فأ مووأ مدقب) ةبسانم... ةيزيلجنإل لا موأ
فسوو	اركش)ةيبرعلاب ىرخأ ةرم اهيلإ رظني) !ةيزيلجنإل لا موأ)ةيزيلجنإلابال) كل.
يلع	لا سوف. انيش. ادحأ يأ يطعي لا ارتلجنإ. هذه هدية. تسيل هذه نركرشب لا تلمعا اذإ – كرجأ نم هذه عطقتأ
فسوو	!!ارتلجنإ)نابابلا لاعفنا)
يلع	.ةينميلا بابلا ةثايلا هذه كرتتنت نأ كيلع
فسوو	؟اذام
يلع	نكنكمي يتلا سبالملا ضعب يدل. انه ةباتنلالاتفلمل ودو ألا لضفأل نم اه. اهترادرا
فسوو	!ارتلجنإ
يلع	يأ ببست الو ,دعتبت لا ."نبرلوه" و "رهنلا نم ابيرق ىقبت كل ينحيحصن رضاح. تقولا يف ام ىرا ىلع عاضيل ىلوألاف. لكاشم
فسوو	؟عاضوأ يأ
يلع	نوكيس فوس نآلا. كترجح كيرأ سوف. هينيح يف ءيش لكل فرعت سوف نوكي دق ,نايحألا ضعب يفو .نيرخآ نيينمي ةثالث عم اهيف شيعلا كيلع كلذ نم ربكأ ددعلا
فسوو	)ةيزيلجنإلاب لوقيو هينه ةقرو جنيه ىلإ ىرخأ ةرم رظني) !ةيزيلجنإ لا مأ
يلع	لكاشملا ضعب كل ببسي دقو. فوسوي اي كل تمدنمو ايغص تلز ام تنأ في "ساواث زدليش".
فسوو	.ةنيدم ةمدقتم ةنيدم تسيل ليم "زدليش ثواس"
يلع	رخآ صخش يأ لثم نوكت نأ بجي ,هابتنالا نكمت لا ,تلتلق امللثم
فسوو	؟رخآ صخش يأ لثم
يلع	هلوقأ ام اذه
فسوو	؟رخآ صخش يأ لثم
يلع	اذه يناببرهك حابصم. هنإ هيتفيو هقلغب مق. انه قلقيو من. يباببهرك حابصم اذه ؟سفنلا هذه ىلع لمعلا يف بغرت له. ةرجحلا
فسوو	.معن

13

علي: ليس هذا هو الأمر يا سهلِ. إن علمي هو الإعتناء بك وتقديمِ الطعام أمامِ المسكن نكن كذلك. وسوف تكسبِ سِوس الذي المالا وكلِ، إليّ تأتي فوف الزلِ ديدِ مدان أنت بما، إليّ به نيّن ما منه ذخ اذا تكن عليكِ يجب أن تكون نوربص رارا. وإذا حدثت أيّ مشاكلا، عليك أن تأتي إليّ. أتفهم؟

يوسف: نعم.

علي: جيداً. مُلسمً نكون فوسو انها. الأمور يري تجرا هكذا كذلك؟

يوسف: بملابس إنجليزية؟

علي: إنّ لتتعلمه الكثير كماك أمأ علمه.

يوسف: مثل لعب الورقِ؟

(ينع يدخل إليه. للنسالبِ تبدو وغربة الملابس أن هاتفرصتبصطح وضحبويب) (الصحف.

ضابط الصحف: السِ حسن جديدِ هنا، هنا إنه لواحِ لظف الساملا فقط.

يوسف: إنني لم آتِ إلى إنجلترا لألعبِ الورقِ.

ضابط الصحف: لقد كانوا يلبِ نورحون أيها العرب على اعتملوا على السفن التي خرجت من زلبلدِ. وقد تغذق مكمِ الزمان زانِ الآنِ. فالذالكِ منهم ديو لو أن مكمِ ترترِ مكِ نوجعون إلى بلادكمِ. و هل مفهم ما أقولِ؟

يوسف: لا. أستطيعُ أن أفهم كلمةً واحدةً مما قلتِ تلق.

ضابط الصحف: انتظرِ. علي أن أبيع بعض الصحفِ. ددع خاصِ! ددع خاصِ! حسم، اقرأ لكل لشيءٍ! السفينة "تايناريموُ" تحطمِ مقمها القايساني في وبور الأطلسِي، *بجانزة قرزة الأزرق* الشريطِ انتزار في الفشلِ اعارا ساعاتِ! بأربع *تعطى لأسرعِ سفن عبرِ تعبر هنية المحيطِ الأطلنطي* من السفينة الألمانية إنها جريدة جريدة *روموسِ ديدرِ جرهرِ يظرِ* خاصِ! ددع الليلايِ النهايِ! "نمن" "بريرِ" ديةِ جريدة مقدمُ وطيةٍ الكلالا جزِ معقلِ بني يا ي "تيتيتِ جازِ زلبلدِ" سينة ستِ ليست ديدرِ وكما هكلها العظمى الطيرانِ بريطِ في امتيانسا جرهة لناسِ للرالِ صفحةٍ بوجودِ تمتعِ أنها إلى الإضافةِ مستعملةِ وردراهِ راءةٍ لشل المثيرةِ. الرسالةِ هذه اقرأ المثيرةِ، يزيزي المحررِ، ...

أعطينا اذا إذا مللاطيطينِ أعداد من ربيرِ العالمِ عنِ نيلتاطانِ تكنكِ ضيفبِ ردرِ قدِ يمكننا، ففي. البرطانية السفنِ على للعملِ البيبِ البشرةِ لأصحابِ الأولويةِ العربِ من كنكه الآلافِ يلي، الحاليِ الوقتِ نومون نمن والصونينِ والهنودِ والعربِ من كنكهِ الآلافِ يلي، الحاليِ الوقتِ أن شكِ لا لندينِ العمالِ عنِ ولولونِ العاطلينِ مهملمهمِ يقوم ويمومِ السفنِ على هناكِ المئاتِ من العربِ الذينِ نيذينِ نون يحررونِ تندينتِ أنتا وهداهِ، الطيبِ ديدِ وامِ الطيبِ نيهِ رارةٍ داخارهِ يستيطيعيونِ بنِ صفِ نصِ لكلِ نولسونِ للرجالِ ولاءِ هؤلاءِ معظمِ أنِ بلةِ، نيهنا. بلِ على العكسِ، انانا رسرِ نخسنِ تدمِ فوتوريفِ فرصِ العملِ للمالاطينِ، وقعِ – وعِ – وعنائعِ. محف مجنمِ لماعِ لماملِ توقعِ

التسجيل؟ يوسف: التسجيل؟ إنه شخصِ في مجنمِ لِ منمعِ يعملِ له هذتبهِ تواحلِ التسجيلِ؟

ضابط الصحف: نعمِ، لتكونِ عاملِ محف على أحواضِ السفنِ. ربرِ بمكنكِ لمحاولةِ. إنها إذا اناِ هو منِ ادخلِ اطيباِ موظفنِ ببطيطِ *(وعدب)* انتظرِ الرسميةِ. الطرطةِ

تفضلت! *(يساعده في حمل المكتب والأدوات الكتابية)* كثير من العمل اليوم. إنه شيء ممل، أليس كذلك؟

الموظف	إن ذلك أمر يشعر بعضنا بالرضى التام.
بائع الصحف	حسنا. لدينا بحار شاب قوي البنية، يريد أن يسجل للعمل.
الموظف	الاسم؟
يوسف	يوسف عبد الله قريش.
الموظف	الجنسية؟
يوسف	إممم – بريطاني!
الموظف	بلد الميلاد؟
يوسف	اليمن.
الموظف	مكان الميلاد؟
يوسف	مق –
بائع الصحف	عدن!
الموظف	مقـ عدن؟
بائع الصحف	لقد ولد في عدن.
يوسف	هل ولدت أنا في عدن؟
الموظف	جواز السفر البريطاني.
يوسف	ماذا؟
الموظف	هل لديك جواز سفر بريطاني؟
بائع الصحف	ليس لديه. وليس لديه شهادة ميلاد. أنت تعرف كيف تسير الأمور في اليمن.
الموظف	*(يكتب)* لا يوجد... جواز السفر.... بي سي 5؟
يوسف	ماذا؟
الموظف	هل لديك نموذج بي سي 5 لتستطيع التسجيل للعمل؟
يوسف	أنا –
بائع الصحف	كيف له أن يشتري نموذج بي سي 5 وهو لم يعمل بعد؟
الموظف	*(يكتب)* لا يوجد... نموذج بي سي 5..
يوسف	هل أبدأ العمل على الفور؟
الموظف	سوف يُوضع الملف مع "الملفات غير المكتملة" طاب يومكم. *(يخرج الموظف).*
يوسف	ما كل هذا؟
بائع الصحف	السيد حسن يمكنه ترتيب كل شيء، نعم السيد حسن *(يدخل علي حسن).*
علي	ربما ليس الأمر سهلا الآن. كن صبوراً يا يوسف. ابق في النُزل. سوف أفعل ما أستطيع فعله.
بائع الصحف	شكرا. اذهب الآن. هناك من هو أفضل منك.

(يخرج علي. تدخل ثيلما وهي ترتدي ملابسها لتخرج للرقص. تمر على يوسف وتقف للحظة. يبدو أن كليهما قد انجذب إلى الآخر. ينظر كلاهما إلى الآخر قبل أن تذهب ثيلما إلى قاعة الرقص. موسيقى راقصة).

ثيلما	إن هذه الموسيقى ترجع بي إلى الوراء. أشعر بأنني غريبة في مكان ما، ويأتي هذا الغريب إليّ ويقول *(يدخل شاب من جيوردي)*
الشاب	هل تحبين الشراب يا جميلة؟
ثيلما	ماذا؟
الشاب	سوف أشتري لك شرابا.
ثيلما	شراب؟ هل تنظر إلى ما حولك؟
الشاب	ماذا تعنين؟
ثيلما	السماء، النهر، البحر، الناس. وهناك تمثال كبير في وسط "نيو كاسل"، إنه " إرلْ جري".
الشاب	أنت لا تحبين الشراب إذًا؟
ثيلما	ألا تفكر أبدا في الهرب؟
الشاب	ماذا تقصدين؟
ثيلما	الهرب من كل شيء.
الشاب	لقد دخلت للتو.
ثيلما	هل تفكر فيّ أيها الشاب الجوردي؟
الشاب	أعتقد ذلك.
ثيلما	تريد أن تتزوجني، وتهب لي العديد من الأطفال، وانشغل بالأطفال وحفاظاتهم لسنوات عشر مقبِلة، هل هذا ما في الأمر؟
الشاب	أنت تقولين أشياء مضحكة، *(يدخل بائع الصحف. يخرج الشاب).*
بائع الصحف	أعتقد أنك كنت تفكرين فيه *(يشير إلى المكان الذي يقف فيه يوسف).*
ثيلما	إنه يبدو مختلفًا قليلا.
بائع الصحف	هل تريدين الارتباط بالعرب؟ ماذا سيقول والدك؟
ثيلما	ماذا يقول دائما؟ *(يدخل جورج).*
جورج	هل لديك أي فكرة كيف كان الوضع عندما غرقت "انفيسيبل" ومعها 1000 رجل؟ والقليل منا متعلق بقطع الخشب وكأننا فنران تغرق، و تجمد الكثير منا ببطء حتى الموت، وقد علّقت قطعة من المعدن بحجم طبق الطعام في رجلي؟ *(تدخل مارجريت).*
مارجريت	تعال يا جورج، سوف أعد لك فنجانا من الشاي.
جورج	ثم العودة إلى الوطن لماذا؟ القتال من أجل بلدك لماذا؟ لا عمل، لا مستقبل.
مارجريت	نعم يا جورج.
ثيلما	إنه يعتريه هذا المزاج، انظر. إنه شيء مخيف.

جورج لا أحد يهتمّ. إنّ زيدلر اللعينة تمتلئ بالعرب الذين يأخذون وظائفنا *(بازدراء)* وهؤلاء الذين يأخذون وظائفنا تمتلئ بهم اللعينة زيدلر. لا شكّ بأنّ هذا القارب، هو الوحيد في *(إلى نموذج القارب الذي صنعه)* شيدلر الذي لا يعمل عليه العرب.

ثيلما إنه يشبه أسطولًا انا لجيل التسجيل في بعض الأحيان.

بائع الصحف ولكنه ليس مثل "جاك هيلتون" بالطبع.

ثيلما لا أعلم. كيف معه بالحياة لا تشعر إلى أمّي. وانظر إلى مثله. لا ليس لا تحتمل ذلك.

مارجريت *(إلى بائع الصحف)* إنه ليس سيئ الخطأه. إنه لا يفهم، لا أحيانًا. وأحيانًا، لا أفهم أنا.

ثيلما هاهي مرة أخرى. دائمًا تقدم له الأعذار.

بائع الصحف لا تضعي الكثير من السكر في الشاي. ففي ذلك ضرر على صحته. رر

مارجريت ليس ضارًا مثل الخمر التي يشربها. والآن يا ثيلما لا تتأخري.

ثيلما قد أخطف. قد أحمل إلى بعض الأراضي البعيدة.

مارجريت لا تتأخري على العاشرة. فلديك عمل في الصباح.

ثيلما لا أستطيع الانتظار راز *(لبائع الصحف)* هل قضيت أيامًا كاملة تنام على قماش الكتان؟

بائع الصحف لقد عشت حياة كريمة.

ثيلما ملاءات مزدوجة، ومقاسات مناسبة. العديد من الوسائد. يكون ذلك جميلًا في بعض الأحيان.

مارجريت سوف يكون الوالد قد أوى إلى فراشه.

ثيلما *(تذهب إلى الرقص مع بعض الأفراد الخياليين).*
إذا ماذا تعمل؟ حسنا اننا نعمل في منجم. ماذا عنك إذًا؟ "بالمرز يارد". نعم. أنت وسيم، بم تحلم؟ تريد أن تلعب وتسجل الأهداف في روكر برك؟ فهمتك. ماذا عنك أيها الفتى النحيف؟ نعم عزيزي، إنه مثل. جذاب جدا. يجب عليك الإعجاب بمن يشرب الكثير. حسنا، في الواقع، إنه لا يستطيع. وأنا لا أعجب به. هذا لكل ما في الأمر.

بائع الصحف معذرة. علي أن أذهب إلى العمل. عدد خاص! عدد خاص! اقرأ كل شيء! عدد خاص! يوم الهدنة! الأمة تكرم موتاها! السياسيون يتعهدون بعدم تكرار الحرب التي لا طائل وراءها! *(يضحك كثيرا)* آسف. لا أستطيع مقاومة ذلك. يتعهدون بعدم تكرار الحرب التي لا طائل وراءها. إن ما نستطيع أن نثق في تعهدهم به، هو أن يقوموا بتلميع الأثاث!

ثيلما يمكنني أن أكون سياسية. يمكنني أن أكون رئيسة وزراء.

بائع الصحف أنت تسبقين كنك يا عزيزتي. انظري، هنا تدخل الآنسة "مارجريت بونونو دليف"، وزيرة العمل، وأول امرأة في مجلس الوزراء.

ثيلما أين؟

بائع الصحف لم تستطع المجيء. الآن، أنت تعرفين القواعد، الزواج ثم الطهو ثم التنظيف ثم التربية.

ثيلما إنك تحب ان تغيض الناس.

بائع الصحف ماذا، مثل الساعة؟

ثيلما ماذا عن ذلك الفتى العربي، أين هو الآن؟

17

الصحف بائع	إنه ينتظر منذ ثلاثة أشهر في النزل. هاهو ، انظري. إنه يلعب الورق ويمضغ القات.

(يذهبان إلى نزل اعمال. يقفز يوسف).

يوسف	*(بالرعب)* يجب أن أحصل على عمل يا سيدي حسن!

علي	إنني لأبذل ما في وسعي.

(نرى علياً ، في عدة مرات، يقدم المسؤول للمال ويقدم يوسف. ويهز المسؤول رأسه . وفي النهاية يأخذ المال). يوسف، لقد حصلت على عمل لك في النهاية، سوف تعمل كعامل فحم على سفينة. كان الله معك.

(يأخذ يوسف الآن دور عامل الفحم، حيث يحمل الفحم إلى المدفأة).

الصحف بائع	*(إليه)* كذلك؟ هل قرأت له؟

(يبدأ في القراءة من مقال في كتاب. يصل إلى نصف المقال ثم تبدأ ثيلما في القراءة).

"يجب أن يقف العامل قرب فوهة الفرن، وينظر إلى الفحم المشتعل داخله، وفي الوقت ذاته، يبحث عن الفحم بسرعة ومهارة ليدخله إلى الفرن، حتى لا يظهر جهاز الكشف للمهندس المراقب أن مستوى البخار يقل.

ثيلما	ولكن تنظيف الحريق لا يعد كونه لعب أطفال. فعندما يزيد العمل، فإن الفرن أو الأفران (لكل عامل فرنان أو ثلاثة يكون مسؤولاً عنها) يجب أن تكون في أوج اشتعالها، ويجب عليهم بذل أقصى ما يستطيعون. ولذلك، يفتح عامل الفحم باب الفرن على مصراعيه لينظفه، ويدخل أداة العمل إلى داخل النار، ويدفع ويرمي ويضرب، حتى يكون شبه مشوي في النار، ويسحب كميات كبيرة من الفحم المحترق *(يأخذ بائع الصحف كتاباً)*.

الصحف بائع	وكل ذلك يبعث بحرارة شديدة إلى أعلى، ثم تكون هناك حاجة إلى تخفيفها، وتصاحب هذه العملية، سحب من البخار والدخان الخانق *(يرجع الكتاب إلى ثيلما).*

ثيلما	ولكن ليل ليس هناك وقت لنضيعه. ومرة وأخرى، فإنه يغوص إلى قلب الفرن في كل مرة لينظفه فيها من بعض الفحم المستعمل، حتى يقذف بمجرفة أخرى من الفحم، في النهاية، بعد أن تكون قد تألمت عيناه، وبعد أن يكون قد اختنق واشتوى، وتعب أشد التعب، ثم يبدأ في إلقاء الفحم في النار الواهنة وير جع في استجماع قوته مرة أخرى. *(ينهار يوسف في النهاية. تتحرك ثيلما لتظهر في المشهد، ولكن بائع الصحف يسحبها إلى الخلف).*

الصحف بائع	إنهم يعدون نوبات كرامة العامل – وهي أسوأ من منع ملاءات السرير *(يدخل بحاران أبيضان).*

الأول البحار	أنت أيها الدول العربي، اغسل هذه الثياب لي *(يرمي بكومة من الملابس إلى يوسف الذي يرميها إليه مرة أخرى)*، ما هذا، أيها العربي المتمرد اللعين؟ انظر إلى ذلك، هذا العربي في رأسه أفكار ترفعه فوق قدره. إنه لا يريد أن يغسل ملابس رجل أبيض. هذا الأسود وقح الحقير *(يبدأ البحار في العراك مع يوسف الذي يطرحه أرضا).*

الأول البحار	سوف تندم على ذلك أيها العربي *(يهاجمه البحاران).*

ثيلما	يوسف! *(تحاول التدخل مرة أخرى. ويمنعها بائع الصحف مرة أخرى).*

الثاني البحار	إنه يوم حظك التعيس أيها العربي. فإذا أخبرنا القبطان، فسوف يكون هذا هو يومك الأخير على هذه السفينة. وسوف ننهي الأمر بذلك، أفهمت؟ *(يهاجمه البحاران ويطرحانه أرضا. يخرج البحاران أرضا. تندفع ثيلما إلى*

18

المشهد وتحاول إراحة يوسف. يأخذها بائع الصحف خارجا، في الوقت الذي يدخل فيه تشارترز).

تشارترز	أيها النادل! (يدخل بائع الصحف).
بائع الصحف	من، أنا؟
تشارترز	كن مرتباً وأحضر لي قائمة الطعام. *(يرتدي بائع الصحف ملابس النادل ويحضر قائمة الطعام إلى تشارترز)* حسناً، بم توصي اليوم من الطعام؟
بائع الصحف	لقد أُعجب الكثيرون بكبد الغنم، المطهو في صلصلة الخردل مع لحم الخنزير المهروس أو المسلوق.
تشارترز	حسنا – لن أختار ذلك مطلقا. ماذا عن الأرانب؟
بائع الصحف	الإقبال عليها أضعف مما اعتدنا عليه بكثير.
تشارترز	ماذا؟
بائع الصحف	إنها خالية من العظم، ومطهوة بالجزر واللفت، مع صلصة التوت، وابتسامة كبيرة.
تشارترز	هل تسخر مني؟
بائع الصحف	ماذا؟ وهل أخاطر بفقدان البقشيش الكبير؟
تشارترز	سوف آخذ شريحة اللحم مع فطيرة الكلى. وأرسل إليّ صديقي إليس من الاتحاد الوطني للبحارة.
بائع الصحف	كيف تحبه يا سيدي؟ مشوي قليلا على الفحم، أم محمص أم مشوي؟
تشارترز	يجدر بك أن تقوم بالتمثيل على المسرح أيها الأحمق الصغير.
بائع الصحف	آه ولكن أنا *(يدخل إليس)* هاهو يا سيدي.
إليس	هل أردت رؤيتي سيد تشارترز؟
تشارترز	إليس، إنني معجب كثيراً بصحيفة الاتحاد الخاصة بكم، ماذا تسمى؟
إليس	البحّار.
تشارترز	إنني لا أحب هذا الاسم إذا أردت رأيي. لا يهم. لقد سمعت أن لها تأثيراً كبيراً.
بائع الصحف	صحيفة البحار. إنها مفاجأة حقا!
إليس	يقرأها كل أعضاء الاتحاد.
بائع الصحف	والآن أعضاء الاتحاد!
تشارترز	إنها وطنية يا إليس؟ تدافع عن البلد؟
بائع الصحف	يقف! ماذا بعد ذلك!
تشارترز	نعم أنت أيها البذيء! ضع جورباً في فمك وأصمت، أتفهم ذلك؟. إليس، أعتقد أنه قد حان الوقت ليكون هناك تعاون مثمر بين الاتحاد الخاص بكم واتحاد الشحن، وأن ننظر إلى أفق تعاون جديد. لقد حان الوقت لكي نقف متحدين وأن نتبنى موقفاً واضحا. هل توافق على ذلك؟
إليس	إن الأمر يعتمد على ما في ذهنك.
تشارترز	ما في ذهني هو افتتاحية في هذه الصحيفة، تجعل الناس واعين بما يحدث من حولهم. اجعلهم يجلسوا ويفكروا، صحيح؟ أليس ذلك هو المقصود من

19

	الصحافة الحرة؟ وأنت يا إليس كرجل أساسي في هذا الاتحاد، يجب أن تكتب هذه الافتتاحية.
بائع الصحف	*(يحضر الطعام)* استمتع بوجبتك يا سيدي.
إليس	أنا ما زلت غير متأكد *(يتحرك تشارترز نحوه ويحادثه سرا)* ألا تعتقد أن ذلك قد يكون فيه بعض الاستفزاز يا سيد تشارترز؟
تشارترز	أسميه استراتيجية أو أسميه تأمينًا.
إليس	ولكن بطريقة ما، فإن ذلك هجوم على بعض الأعضاء.
تشارترز	في بعض الأحيان يجب عليك أن تكون شجاعا، أليس كذلك؟ والآن دعنا نرى كيف يمكنك أن تكون كاتبًا بارعا. *(يقدم قلما وورقة. يكتب إليس الافتتاحية ويقدمها إلى تشارترز عن طريق بائع الصحف)* جيد جدا يا إليس. فلتتناول بطاطا مسلوقة.
بائع الصحف	ربما يجب علي أن أقرأ أن ذلك سيد تشارترز. فلديك ما يكفي من فطيرة اللحم في طبقك.
تشارترز	حسنا. يبدو الأمر واضحا الآن.
بائع الصحف	*(في الوقت الذي يقرأ فيه، تدخل شخصيات المسرحية لتستمع)* "يجب أن نفهم أننا لا نعترض على هؤلاء العرب، ولكن المساعدة تبدأ من الداخل، وباستبعاد هؤلاء الرجال، الذين سيكونون في وضع أفضل إذا عادوا إلى بلادهم، فسوف تكون هناك فرص وظيفية، ليس فقط لعمال الفحم المستبعدين، ولكن لعمال الفحم السابقين كذلك، وسوف يتمكن البحارة السابقون من العودة إلى عملهم. فهؤلاء إذا تم تسريحهم، فسوف يكونون عبئا جديدا على سوق العمل التي تعاني من البطالة بالفعل."
تشارترز	إنها كلمة جيدة.
جورج	ولها مغزى ى جيد جدا.
علي	ولكن ذلك يصعب الأمور على كل البحارة العرب!
تشارترز	*(إلى بائع الصحف)* وبالنسبة لك، فمن الأفضل لك أن تحضر ملعقة حلوى نظيفة. فهذه الملعقة قذرة جدا. *(يخرج وذراعه حول إليس)* إن الصحافة الحرة شيء رائع يا إليس. أعتقد......
بائع الصحف	عدد خاص! عدد خاص! اقرأ كل شيء! سفينة نرويجية تتحطم على صخور "بلاك ميدن"، وسط ضباب كثيف ـلم يمت أحد!
	(يأخذنا ذلك إلى نُزل العمال، حيث يلعب الأصدقاء الورق ويمضغون القات. يجري هذا المشهد باللغة العربية مع ترجمة كتابية للإنجليزية).
علي	هل أنت غبي يا يوسف؟
يوسف	لا!
علي	إذا طلب منك رجل أبيض أن تغسل له ثيابه، فاغسلها.
يوسف	ليس أنا من يفعل ذلك!
علي	اليمنيون أناس طيبون. لا يعادون الآخرين.
يوسف	عليك أن تفتح عينيك.
علي	عم تتحدث؟
يوسف	أنت أعمى – افتح عينيك!

20

علي	إنني أبذل قصارى جهدي لصالح البحارة، لكل الجمعيع، الاثني عشر. معي.
يوسف	وماذا عن نفسك؟
علي	ماذا تعني بذلك؟ *(إلى بائع الصحف بالإنجليزية)* ماذا يعني بذلك؟
بائع الصحف	برب العربة. يعني بما أنك تعيش حياة صعبة بسبب عنايتك بالبحارة الاثني عشر.
علي	أكبر منك إنين! هذا شيء مهم، أنت لا تحترم من هم أكبر منك *(يرى مرة أخرى بالعربي)* انس.

يوسف	*(إلى بائع الصحف بالإنجليزية)* أنت يني أخبره *(خرج فوف يسني أخبره)* أخرج!
علي	*(بالإنجليزية)* إنه مسلم سيء جيداً!
يوسف	*(بالإنجليزية)* جيد، إنني مسلم جيد، ولكنني سوف أخرج!
علي	*(بالعربية)* أين ستذهب يا نوني؟
يوسف	أين أنا الآن؟ *(يترك يوسف المنزل. يقابله ثليما في الشارع).*
ثليما	كيف حال عينك؟
يوسف	إنها تتشافى. شكراً لك.
ثليما	قيقيش ورطيف أنت.
يوسف	في اليمن، معظم الناس شريقون.
ثليما	معظم الشباب هنا لديهم بطن كبير من شرب الخمر.
يوسف	من شرب الخمر؟
ثليما	لا تشغل بالك. اسمي ثليما نتشارلتون.وأستطيع أن أحصل لك على غرفة مصص عشرة بالمنة عند شدة ملاءات السرير في "بنس".
يوسف	ماذا تقولين؟
ثليما	لا يهم. ما اسمك؟
يوسف	اسمي يوسف عبد الله قريش.
ثليما	هذا لطيف. أنت من اليمن، أليس كذلك؟ يمكنك أن تذهب بي إلى هناك.
يوسف	اليمن بلد سيء، وحكامه سيئون. والناس هناك في شدة الفقر. إن إنجلترا هي بلدي الآن.
ثليما	لقد انتهت إنجلترا. ما اسم كتابكم المقدس؟
يوسف	إنه القرآن الكريم.
ثليما	هل هو جيد؟
يوسف	إنه كلام الله التي نقلها إلينا نبيه محمد – صلى الله عليه وسلم.
ثليما	ليس مثل كتب أجاثا كريستي إذاً؟
يوسف	أوروق يقرؤه المسلم لك.
ثليما	معظمنا يقرأ جريدة الجازيت. ويحك، هل تعلم أن "وليم بويد" يمثل في فيلم *"الرقاب الجلدية"* في سينما "جراند إلكتريك"، هذا الأسبوع؟
يوسف	أنا آسف. لا أفهمك.

21

الميث	حسناً يا يوسف. هل كنت تعيش في مدينة إذاً؟
يوسف	مقبنة – مكان يتميز بالجبال العالية.
الميث	يبدو أمراً لطيفاً. لا شك أن هناك الكثير من الماعز والخراف والخنازير.
يوسف	ماعز وخراف نعم. جبن وعسل. ولكن لا يوجد هناك خنازير.
الميث	أحب أكل بعض العسل هناك عالياً على أحد الجبال.
يوسف	إنها حياة شديدة الفقر. لقد أتيت إلى إنجلترا من أجل الحضارة.
الميث	الحضارة؟ ويحك – قل ذلك مرة أخرى.
يوسف	ماذا؟
الميث	اسم المكان الذي كنت تعيش فيه.
يوسف	مقبنة.
الميث	مقبنة! لا شك أنهم ما يزالون لا يعرفون السينما في مقبنة.
يوسف	السينما؟
الميث	إنها في كل مكان الآن يا يوسف. أحب "جاري كوبر" و"جريتا جاربو".
يوسف	أنت جميلة جدا، ولكنك تتحدثين عن أشياء غريبة.
الميث	يمكنني أن آخذك إلى هناك.
يوسف	أين؟
الميث	إلى السينما! جراند إلكتريك. القصر. بافليون. آه، قل إنك سوف تأتي.
يوسف	أنا وأنت. وسوف يأتي والداك كذلك؟
الميث	بالطبع لا! انظر. أريد أن أفعل ذلك *(تقبله)* ألا تحب ذلك؟
يوسف	هذه الأشياء لا تحدث في اليمن.
الميث	وهي لا تحدث في شيلدز بالقدر الكافي، إلا مع الرجال الذين لا يقدرونها. هل يمكن أن تعيرني كتابك؟
يوسف	لا أستطيع أن أعيرك إياه، لا.
الميث	يمكن أن أشتري نسخة خاصة بي إذاً.
يوسف	القرآن للمسلمين فقط.
الميث	أجاثا كريستي للجميع *(تقبله مرة أخرى).*
يوسف	أشعر بدوار الآن.
الميث	أنا كذلك. الأسبوع القادم إذاً. يمكننا أن نذهب للشراب في "إيجل" أولاً.
يوسف	المسلمون لا يشربون.
الميث	رجال لا يشربون؟ لا يمكن أن تجد الكثير مثلك هنا في ساوث شيلدز ! . هل لديك أي موسيقى يا بائع الصحف؟
بائع الصحف	هاهي! *(موسيقى).*
الميث	تعال إذاً *(يرقصان)* الرقص هو الحياة يا يوسف. إنه هو الذي يشعرني بالحياة. عندما أرقص لا يهمني أي شيء آخر. ويحك، إنك ماهر

22

بطبيعتك، ولديك إعاقة! ((تقترب أنثى الراقص)، إذا أنت لم تقتبِل أي فتاة إنجليزية من قبل؟

يوسف لم أقبِّل أي فتاة من قبل. أما يا أخي وأختي فقط.

ثيلما هذا أمر مختلف.

يوسف معم. أحب التقبيل الإنجليزي (يقبّلها).

ثيلما ربما لم تجرب ذلك من قبل، لا – آه، لا أقصد الإساءة بالطبع إ!

يوسف لم أجرب؟

ثيلما لا يهم.

يوسف أريد أن أعرف كل شيء. وأجرب كل شيء.

ثيلما وأنا كذلك. ربما أتيت من اليمين لتقابلني.

يوسف ربما.

ثيلما لماذا سافرت هذه المسافة من اليمن، لكي تعمل في ساوث سيلدز فقط؟

بائع الصحف ربما أستطيع تقديم المساعدة هنا.

ثيلما آه، ربما أنت تعرف كل شيء.

بائع الصحف يمكنك أن تقولي ذلك.

ثيلما حسن – ما هي أعلى قمة جبل ثاني في العالم؟

بائع الصحف جبل يسمى "كاي 2" ويبلغ طوله 28.250 قدما.

ثيلما أنت مثقّف جدا.

بائع الصحف أعرف كذلك لماذا يأتي اليمنيون ليعملوا في ساوث سيلدز.

ثيلما أتعقّد كأنك سوف تخبرنا.

بائع الصحف يصور المشهد. هنا. في يناير من عام 1839. يدخل ضابط بحري إنجليزي يحرر *(بائع الصحف يرتقي إلى رتبة عالية. ذو (يدخل الضابط).*

الضابط البحري أنت هناك! أنت أيها البحار! رتب بنفسك! *(بائع الصحف يرتدي ملابس* مناسبة للبحرية) تحرك، كف، تعال! ألا تريد البحرية؟ أليس كذلك، خبير، البحرية أساس... الآن؟ إذا له كيف يمكنك رتر أن ميناء عدن؟ *(يخرج بائع الصحف ويرجع حاملا ضخما.*

بائع الصحف أستأنف التلسكوب *(ينظر عبر التلسكوب يسمى به)* نعم يا سيدي! أرى أن عدن يا سيدي!

الضابط البحري إنها الميناء اليمن. بلد من جزء هائل إلى الاحتلال. هذه الميناء باسم التاج البريطاني حتى في الحال.

بائع الصحف نعم سيدي!

الضابط البحري الولاة أوقرسيل سفينة بحري لديدم كانت الأيام هؤلاء هي فينة بريطانية يسيرون لمهمتهم إلى ألى نقلنا حاجة في درسا.

بائع الصحف نعم سيدي! له هذا هو السبب الحقيقي للاحتلال عدن يا سيدي؟

الضابط البحري ماذا؟

بائع الصحف أما أذكر يا سيدي، هنا قد مر عامان على سرقة السفينة.

الضابط البحري هل تحاول التمرد؟

23

بائع الصحف	بالطبع لا يا سيدي! فليبارك الرب الملكة فيكتوريا يا سيدي، وكل من يبحر باسمها يا سيدي! ولكنني ظننت أنه يمكن أن أذكر كيف أن بريطانيا العظمى تحتاج بشدة إلى محطة تزود بالوقود بين بومباي والسويس، يا سيدي، ويبدو أن عدن هي المكان الملائم لذلك تماما يا سيدي. وأسف يا سيدي.
الضابط البحري	عليك أن تتحلى بالصمت إزاء ما لا تفهمه، إذا لم تكن ترغب في العقاب.
بائع الصحف	بالطبع يا سيدي، سوف أحتل عدن على الفور يا سيدي! لكنني ظننت أنه يمكنني يا سيدي أن أذكر أن هناك بعض الفتيان ــ ليس أنا بالطبع يا سيدي ــ ممن يعتقدون أن احتلال عدن قد يكون لحرمان مصر من احتلال جنوب الجزيرة العربية، وأن تصبح خطرا على التوسع البريطاني يا سيدي!.
الضابط البحري	قم بالمهمة! فلتحتل عدن!.
بائع الصحف	على الفور يا سيدي! *(يقوم بُنلك)،* لقد أحتلت عدن يا سيدي! الآن أصبحت منطقة بريطانية *(يرفرف العلم فوقها)* مما يجعل كل مولود في عدن يا سيدي ينتمي إلى الجنسية البريطانية ويحمل جواز السفر البريطاني وغير ذلك من الفوائد يا سيدي! إئذن لي يا سيدي في أن أنقل كل شيء نصف قرن إلى المستقبل، وأن أغيرك من ضابط بحري استعماري إلى شريف شحن ناجح يا سيدي!.
الضابط البحري	حسنا لك الإذن.
	(يصيح شريفا. ويصيح بائع الجرائد ضابطا بحريا).
الشريف	الآن يا ضابط البحرية، نحن نفتقر إلى عدد من العمال على القوارب، أليس كذلك؟
بائع الصحف	نعم، نعم، نحن كذلك يا سيدي. إن العمل ينمو بسرعة كبيرة، وليس لدينا ما يكفي من البحارة.
الشريف	يجب علينا أن نجد موردا جديدا إذا. وقد سمعت أن كل هؤلاء العرب جيدون في العمل.
بائع الصحف	نعم يا سيدي إنهم مجدون في العمل ويمكن الاعتماد عليهم.
الشريف	وهم هادئون مثلما سمعت.
بائع الصحف	إنهم لا يثيرون أي مشاكل يا سيدي.
الشريف	ليسوا مثل عمالنا؟ أليس كذلك؟ فمعظم عمالنا يدمنون الشراب بمجرد وصولهم إلى الشاطئ، ويظلون يشربون، حتى عندما يرجعون إلى السفن. هذا إذا رجعوا إليها. يمكننا أن نعمل مع هؤلاء العرب، فهناك الكثير من العمل في كارديف، وليفربول وساوث شيلدز. هؤلاء اليمنيون ــ إذا وقعوا وثائقهم في عدن، يمكنهم الحصول على الجنسية البريطانية. وهذا يجعل الأمر سهلا.
بائع الصحف	حتى إذا لم يأتوا من عدن؟
الشريف	إنه مجرد قانون لعين. فإذا كانت لديهم أي مسحة عقل، فإنهم سوف يقولون إنهم إنما أتوا من عدن.
بائع الصحف	ليست لدى هؤلاء العرب الخبرة الكافية في العمل على السفن يا سيدي.
الشريف	اجعلهم يعملون كعمال فحم. لا يجب أن تكون أمير لتلقي بالفحم إلى الفرن.

24

بائع الصحف	على الفور يا سيدي. تعالوا هنا أيها الفتيان، من هنا الآن. نعم هنا. تحركوا يا فتيان. نعم هكذا، هذا صحيح. جيد جدا. اعملوا بهذه الطريقة. *(يخرج الشريف ويرجع بائع الصحف إلى طبيعته. يتحدث إلى ثيلما)* آسف، هل كنت تقولين شيئا؟
ثيلما	كنت أقول كيف سأذهب أنا ويوسف إلى السينما. إنك لم تذهب إلى هناك من قبل يا يوسف، أليس كذلك؟
يوسف	هناك الكثير مما لم أفعله.
ثيلما	هيا إذا *(بلههبان إلى السينما ويجلسان معا)* انظر ــ هذا "راندولف سكوت". إنه وسيم، أليس كذلك؟ وكذلك أنت يا يوسف. إنها ابتسامتك. هل يمكن أن تكون مشهورا؟
يوسف	هل تعتقدين أنه يمكنني أن أكون مشهورا؟

(يدخل شارب في جانب من المسرح).

شارب	لم لا يا بني؟ إنك ماهر جدا بقبضتيك. هل تذكر هذا الرجل الذي أوقعته على السفينة؟ أعتقد أنك رجل قوي حقا.
يوسف	من أنت؟
شارب	اسمي شارب. إنني أبحث دائما عن ملاكم جديد.
يوسف	ملاكم؟
شارب	إنها المهارة يا بني. عادة ما يكون اليمنيون الهادئون هم الأفضل. والملاكم الجيد يمكن أن يكتشف. إنه عمل مُكسب.

(يدخل تريمدون إلى الجانب الآخر من المسرح).

تريمدون	اسمي تريمدون أخي يوسف. لقد كونت فرع شيلدز لحركة البحارة الأقلية. لقد دافعت عن حقوق العمال على هذا القارب.
يوسف	إذا؟
تريمدون	نحن نحارب من أجل حقوق البحارة. بغض النظر عن لونهم أو جنسهم. لقد باعنا الاتحاد الوطني للبحارة. أريد منك الظهور على الرصيف معي في "ميل دام" الأسبوع المقبل. فلنتضامن معا.
ثيلما	هلا ذهبت؟ نحن نشاهد الفيلم.
تريمدون	هناك أشياء أكثر أهمية من الأفلام في هذه الحياة يا عزيزتي.
ثيلما	أنا لست عزيزتك.
تريمدون	هل تعلم أن الاتحاد الوطني للبحارة جناح يميني رجعي يخون أعضاءه العرب ويتآمر مع أصحاب السفن ليجبرونهم على ترك العمل؟
ثيلما	أعتقد أننا نفقد أحسن جزء في الفيلم.
شارب	سوف أعقد معك اتفاقا يا بني. أنت تحتفظ بأربعين بالمئة من الأرباح. إنها ليست قواعد لعبة الملاكمة، وهناك بعض العقبات. ماذا تقول؟
ثيلما	أقول اذهبا أنتما الاثنان. نحن في موعد غرامي.
شارب	ماذا تقول يا بني؟
تريمدون	أخي يوسف؟
يوسف	أنا ــ
ثيلما	يوسف.

25

يوسف	لقد جئت هنا لأشاهد "راندولف سكوت". ولكي أحصل على قبلة إنجليزية.
	(يقبّل ثيلما وتقبّله).
شارب	أراك لاحقًا إذا، اتفقنا؟
تريمدون	عندما تنتهي من ذلك إذا يا أخي يوسف.
	(يخرج الاثنان).
ثيلما	شكرًا لك يا يوسف. سوف تكون الأمور على ما يرام، سوف ترى.
يوسف	نعم كل شيء سوف يكون على ما يرام.
	(يدخل بائع الصحف. يقبّلان بعضهما مرة أخرى).
بائع الصحف	عدد خاص! عدد خاص! النهائي الليلة. رابطة الأمم تحتفل بذكراها العاشرة. اقرأ كل شيء! السماح بتدخين النساء في الأماكن العامة – حديث السيدة "أستور"! عدد خاص! عدد خاص! أنتما الاثنان، لقد انتهى الفيلم. حان وقت الرجوع!

(يخرج يوسف وثيلما. يغادر بائع الصحف المسرح وحده. ينظر حوله للحظات، ثم ينادى من جانب المسرح).
السيدة تشارلتون – تعالي هنا وقدمي القصة إذا لم يكن لديك مانع *(تدخل مارجريت).*

مارجريت	لا يجب أن يمثّل ذلك مشكلة يا جورج *(يدخل جورج).*
جورج	لا يجب أن يمثّل ذلك مشكلة؟ ابنتنا ثيلما مع العربي الوقح؟
مارجريت	إنه اختيارها.
جورج	وما العيب في فتيان شيلدز؟
مارجريت	لا أعرف، أعني – *(تدخل ثيلما).*
ثيلما	أحبه يا أبي.
جورج	نعم، ماذا؟
ثيلما	أحب يوسف.
جورج	هذا أمر مفاجئ بالنسبة لي.
ثيلما	إنك لم تره من قبل.
جورج	إنني أراه في كل مرة أذهب فيها إلى "ميل دام" ، يبحث عن عمل. وأقابله في كل مرة يعطون فيها عملاً لبعض العرب، ولا أجد أنا العمل.
ثيلما	ولكنك يا أبي لست بصحة جيدة، و-
جورج	صحتي جيدة وتؤهلني للعمل على القوارب. إنني كأي عربي.
مارجريت	لا أريد منك أن تزعج نفسك يا جورج.
ثيلما	سوف أحضره إلى هنا.
جورج	ماذا؟
ثيلما	إلى هذا المنزل. سوف أحضر يوسف. أريده أن يقابلني مع أبي وأمي.
جورج	يا للأسف.
مارجريت	ثيلما، لا أعتقد أن هذه فكرة جيدة و-

المليم	أنا لست خجولة به يا أمي. أنا فخورة به. أنا لا أخبئه بعيدا عنكما.
مارجريت	بالطبع لا يا عزيزتي، ولكن-
جورج	تريدين إحضار بحار عربي هنا؟!
المليم	من الأفضل لكما أن تعتادا على الفكرة، كلاكما.
جورج	لقد فقدت عقلها.
مارجريت	المليم-
المليم	ليس عليك أن تأخذي الأمور ببساطة يا أمي مثلما تفعلين دائما. يجب عليك أن ترحبي بيوسف، هل تسمعين؟ حاولي ألا تسترضي أبي ولو لمرة واحدة يا أمي.
مارجريت	سوف أفكر في ذلك!
المليم	نعم يا أمي، لماذا لا تفعلين ذلك؟.

(تخرج المليم. ينظر جورج ومارجريت إلى بعضهما. ثم يتجه إلى نموذج قاربه، يدخل بائع الصحف).

بائع الصحف	نموذجه هذا – لقد أخذ الفكرة من ورشة "بيلي بوي" في جريدة الجازيت. وربما ينهيه في يوم من الأيام. لا تندهش رغم ذلك. هنا يا علي، سوف ألعب الورق من أجلك. هيا نوزع الورق، حسنا؟ هيا يا يوسف، ركز معي.
علي	*(إلى بائع الصحف)* هل تعرف كيف تلعب الورق؟
بائع الصحف	أنا أعرف كل شيء *(بالعربية).*
علي	إنه لا يجيد اللعب، يوسف –
بائع الصحف	يمكنك أن تقول أن عقله في مكان آخر *(بالعربية).*
علي	نعم. مع هذه البنت البيضاء *(يوزع الأوراق وهو يتحدث. يتجمع آخرون حولهم)* أنت شريكي في اللعب يا يوسف، هيا الآن. لا، كان يجب أن تختار القلوب لتربح، لأن معك ورقة الفوز. أنت معك الورقة الرابحة، تذكر. العب مع شريكك.
يوسف	أنا آسف.
علي	حسنا جدا. إلعب. لا. الآن لأن القلوب ليست أوراقا فائزة، فإن أمير القلوب يحسب باثنين فقط وليس بعشرين. استمر في اللعب.
يوسف	أنا آسف. أنا أحبها، ولكن ليس لدي مال. هل يمكنك أن تصلح هذا الأمر؟
علي	هناك القليل من العمل للعرب الآن. عدم وجود نموذج "بي سي 5 " يجعل الأمور صعبة. ليس الأمر ممكنا دائما.

(يقوم يوسف ويخرج خارج النزل. يقابل شارب. ينظر كلاهما للآخر. يدخل بائع الصحف).

بائع الصحف	انتظر – إنني أشعر بأن أحدهم سوف يطلبني الآن. *(يدخل تشارلترز. مغطي بالصابون استعدادا للحلاقة).*
تشارترز	الآن، أين هذا الحلاق الوقح؟
بائع الصحف	*(يضع معطف الحلاق)* هنا يا سيدي!

27

تشار ترز	أريد أن تكون بشرتي ناعمة مثل مؤخرة الطفل. حسناً واحذر ما تفعله بهذه الموسى *(يساعده الحلاق على الاستعداد للحلاقة ويبدأ في عمله)* تعال يا إليس *(يدخل إليس)* يمكنك أن تحلق بنفسك. أو اجعل هذا الفتى يحلق لك. يمكنك أن تفعل ذلك على حسابي.
إليس	إنها حركة البحارة الأقلية يا سيد تشار ترز.
تشارترز	ما هذه؟؟
إليس	إنهم يسببونبونون الكثير من الشغب في ساوث شيلدز. ويثيرون المشاكل.
تشارترز	هذا ما يفعله الشيوعيون دائماً. هذا ما يعيشون من أجله. أيها الحلاق ولو قح. ماذا كانت مهنتك السابقة؟ هل كنت تقطع الأشجار؟.
بائع الصحف	لقد كنت حانوتياً يا سيدي!
تشارترز	هل تمزح؟
بائع الصحف	لقد كنت أهتم بالموتى. هل تعرف ذلك؟ وكنت أكفن بعض القتلى كذلك. نعم القتلى!
إليس	إنهم يحاولون أن يجعلوا كل البحارة يقاطعون المراكب، ويحاولون إلغاء نموذج بي سي 5.
تشارترز	ماذا؟! البيض مع العرب ولماذا يعملون ذلك؟
إليس	نعم، هذا ما يقال.
تشارترز	سوف يكون ذلك من سوء الحظ. أعتقد أننا قد فعلنا ما فيه الكفاية لمنع ذلك من الحدوث. أيها الحلاق ولوقح، أنت لا تقص أعشاباً هنا!.
بائع الصحف	آسف يا سيدي.
تشارترز	هل ستقول أن لدي ذقناً كبيرا؟
بائع الصحف	ذقن كبير؟ آه لا، ليس كذلك مطلقاً يا سيدي!
تشارترز	على أي حال يا إليس، سوف يواجهون مشاكل أكثر من نموذج بي سي 5 قريبا.
إليس	هل تقصد مظام العمل الجديد؟
تشارترز	إنه يطبق جيداً في "أنتويريرب". وقد تم تطبيقه بعد تقييم كامل من السوق وهيئة الصناعة.
إليس	لقد علمت أنه قد طبق ليعاقب البحارة العرب.
تشارترز	لماذا نفعل ذلك كله الآن؟
إليس	سوف يكون للبيض ضلوية أولوية العمل. وهذه ميزة واضحة لهم.
تشارترز	إذا قابلت كلبين نينين غاضبين يا إليس، ماذا ستفعل؟
إليس	كلبين نينين غاضبين؟
تشارترز	تأكد من أنهما يمسكان بعنق بعضهما وليس عنقك.
إليس	لقد كنت متعاوناً أناً قدر استطاعتي مع اتحاد الشحن يا سيد تشار ترز.
تشارترز	سوف يكون من الأفضل أن يكون هناك المزيد من رجال الاتحاد مثلك. يا ليتك أيها الحلاق تتمتع بالمهارة في عملك.
بائع الصحف	لن تعرفك السيدة تشارترز عندما أنتهي يا سيدي.

28

تشاراترز	نعم، يمكن لنا أن نحلم. كم تأخذ مقابل تقطيع ربيعتي هكذا أيها الخلاق؟
بائع الصحف	إنه سعر معقول جدا يا سيدي. يمكنك أن تقول إنه رخيص جدا.
تشاراترز	اغرب عن وجهي إذا

(يقف ويعطي بائع الصحف بعض النقود).

بائع الصحف	هذا أمر غير رائع بالملمرة *(يخرج).*
تشاراترز	حرك بائع الصحف بمسيرات واحتياجات توم الآلية. إذا غضب الناس يا إلي، فإنهم قد يحتاجون إلى هدف للتنفيس عن هذا الغضب. قد يشعرون بالخذلان أو الخيانة. وقد يذهبون في اتجاه الآلات الخطأ أحيانا. ما الأمر إذا؟ أنت *(إلى بائع الصحف)* قم بتشغيل بعض الموسيقى الوطنية.
بائع الصحف	على الفور يا سيدي!

(أغنية تشب هناك تكون فوس "سابها دائما" تذكر تشاراترز والده وهو يربي زي البحارة القديم).

الوالد	لقد كنت فخورا بارتدائي هذه الملابس. كنت فخورا بالحرب في سبيل الملك والوطن. كنت فخورا بالذهاب إلى هذه البحار البعيدة.
تشاراترز	أنت رجل صالح، رجل طيب.
الوالد	أنا رجل منسي.
تشار	منسي؟ لا – لا إن الوطن مدين لك.
الوالد	لقد قالوا إب بي في سلة المهملات.
تشاراترز	كلنا نعمل ما نستطيع حول الأشياء هلكه انظر. حول ما نستطيع تغيره.
الوالد	إنني أحب ما أرى.
تشاراترز	لرجل مثلك هم هم. لقد قدم لك عماد هذا البلد. لقد أخذوا منك شيء لكنه شيء لش مهين. أن ترى الآخرين يأخذون منك لك شيء.

نهاية الفصل الأول

29

الفصل الثاني

(يدخل بائع الصحف)

بائع الصحف	النهائي الليلة! إصدار صحيفة القناة! رفض العرض! عدد خاص! عدد خاص!، إلى أين تذهب يا يوسف؟

(يدخل يوسف)

يوسف	أحاول الحصول على عمل بنفسي *(يذهب ليسجل، ويدخل الموظف)*.
الموظف	آسف، لا يوجد عمل.
يوسف	الكثير من الرجال يسجلون للعمل على السفينة "كيب فيرد".
الموظف	آسف.
يوسف	الكثير من الرجال البيض. لماذا لا أستطيع أنا؟
بائع الصحف	اقرأ ذلك.

(يقرأ من صحيفة شيلدز جازيت).

عزيزي المحرر،

إنك تقول إن العرب مساوون للإنجليز – ولا أدري هل أضحك أم أجن، عندما أفكر فيما تقوله. لماذا؟ لأنهم ليسوا بريطانيين، بل إنه لا تبلغ نسبة البريطانيين فيهم أكثر من عشرة بالمئة. وبالنسبة لشجاعتهم في الحروب، فلا يمكننا أن نقول بذلك، لأنه بناء على خبرتي وخبرة أصدقائي، فإن نصفهم قد مات رعباً قبل أن يبتعلهم البحر. وبالنسبة لاتحاد البحارة فقد كونه بحارة وعمال فحم بيض رعباً قبل أن يبتعلهم البحر. وبالنسبة لاتحاد البحارة فقد ويحرموا الرجال البيض من العمل والكسب. إنني متأكد من أننا لن نفلس إذا ذهب هؤلاء العرب بعيدا. إن نصيحتي لهؤلاء –بما أنهم لا يفهمون ذلك– هو أنهم غير مرغوبين في هذا البلد. وعلاوة على ذلك، فإنني لا أشعر بالحب تجاه العرب فقط، ولكنني أكرههم أيضا.

توقيع بوجو

(ربما يكون هناك صدى للجملة الأخيرة. يبتعد يوسف ويبحث عن شارب، ويمد يديه. يفحص شارب قبضتيه، ويطلب منه خلع قميصه. لدينا اليوم مباراة في الملاكمة. يدخل هاري).

هاري	هل تعد عربياً للنزال؟ إنهم لا يعرفون شيئا عن ذلك.
شارب	نعم، حسنا. فقط ضع مالك حيث يجب يا "هاري والتن".

(يتقدم الآن خصم أبيض ويبدأ النزال. يلعب يوسف ببراعة أمام الرجل الآخر. تقوم شخصيات أخرى من المسرحية بدور المشجعين. وفي النهاية، يضع شارب أموالاً في يد يوسف. يخرج هو والآخرون ويتركون يوسف وثيلما).

ثيلما	هل هذا جرح فوق عينك؟ *(تنظر إليه)* هل تفعل ذلك من أجلي يا يوسف؟
يوسف	يجب أن أكون رجلاً من أجلك.
ثيلما	أنت رجل بالفعل. هل ستأتي إلى منزلنا؟
يوسف	منزلكم؟

ثيلما	لن يكون هناك لحم خنزير *(يدخل شارب)*.
شارب	يوسف *(نزال أخر. تتكرر الأحداث ويفوز يوسف)*. إنهم يصطفون ليحاولوا هزيمة يوسف. أنت جيد في عملك يا يوسف. أنت جيد جدا لجلب الربح.
يوسف	*(إلى ثيلما)* هل سيكون كل شيء على ما يرام؟
ثيلما	كان والدي قليلا – أنت تعرف. ولكنه الآن يقول لا بأس. أنا وأنت يا يوسف سوف نكون معا. فكيف لا تكون الأمور على ما يرام؟ ويحك، إنك جيد جدا.
شارب	إنه ملاكم بالفطرة يا عزيزتي. وكأنه قد ولد ليصبح ملاكما.
ثيلما	لقد ولد من أجلي. لقد جاء من أجلي ومعه كتابه.

(تشاهد وهو يتظاهر بالملاكمة. إنه يبدو بارعا فيها تماما. وفي الوقت الذي كان يحدث فيه ذلك، كان تريمدون قد أحضر صندوقا صغيرا في مكان آخر على المسرح ووقف عليه، ودعا الناس حوله).

تريمدون	دعوني أقرأ لكم أيها الإخوة في مقاطعة "تاينسايد" من الحزب الشيوعي في بريطانيا العظمى *(يقرأ)* إن البحارة يكافحون هذا التحالف الثلاثي لملاك السفن، الحكومة العمالية، واتحاد البحارة الفاشي، والإتحاد الوطني للبحارة. ولكي نحطم ذلك التحالف وننتصر، يجب على البحارة أن يتخذوا إجراءات قوية وأن يحطموا سياسة المقاومة السلبية. يجب أن نتخذ موقفا فاعلا لمنع الحقيرين من التسجيل وهزيمة كفاحكم – لا يمكننا عمل ذلك بالمقاومة السلبية – لن يقوم أي بحار بالعمل في اتحاد الشحن أو مكاتب الاتحاد الوطني للبحارة حتى تلبى جميع طلباتنا من قبل اتحاد الشحن ومالكي السفن. لقد فشلت المقاومة السلبية في وقف أي سفينة عن العمل، ومن شأن ذلك أن يوضح لنا فشل وخطورة هذه السياسة. علينا أن نمنع التسجيل بفعالية وأن نمنع كل السفن من العمل وأن ندعو كل البحارة في كل الموانى ليتوقفوا عن العمل. *(ينظر إلى يوسف)* هل ستنضم إلينا أخي يوسف؟ هل ستقاتل؟
يوسف	إنني أقاتل *(يتظاهر بالملاكمة على المسرح في اتجاه علي)*.
علي	الرجال البيض غاضبون من يوسف.
يوسف	الكل غاضبون.
علي	حتى البحارة اليمنيون.
يوسف	يجب علي أن أذهب. لدي موعد هام.

(يخرج علي. تدخل ثيلما. ويستعد يوسف لمقابلة العائلة).

ثيلما	إنني قلقة بعض الشيء يا يوسف. هل أنت كذلك؟
يوسف	أنا بخير. الله معي.
ثيلما	أنت لا تعرف ما معنى أن يوافق أبي على مقابلتك.
يوسف	أنا واثق من أن أباك رجل طيب.
بائع الصحف	*(يدخل ومعه باقة زهور)* ويحك – خذ هذه!
يوسف	ماذا؟!
بائع الصحف	إلى السيدة تشارلتون.
يوسف	شكرا لك.

ثيلما	لا شك أن الإيمان شيء جيد يا يوسف.
يوسف	أليس لديك إيمان؟
ثيلما	لا يهتم الكثير منا بالكنيسة وهذه الأشياء. فهي لحفلات الزفاف والمآتم، هذا ما تعني بالنسبة لنا. هذه الزهور رائحتها جميلة. ما حدث لوالدي هو أنه كان على قاربه عندما انفجر وغرق في الحرب. لقد غرق الكثير من الرجال. وقد جرح حينئذ وأصيب بالعرج منذ ذلك الوقت. لم يعد كما كان، ولم يستطع العمل ثانية على مراكب شيلدز.
يوسف	وهو يلوم العرب عل ذلك.
ثيلما	نوعًا ما. شكرا على مجيئك يا يوسف.
يوسف	يجب علي أن أعرف كل شيء عنك يا ثيلما. إنني رجل محظوظ. في اليمن، يقوم الآخرون بترتيب هذه الأشياء.
ثيلما	سوف ندخل الآن. قبلني ومن ثم سندخل *(يقبلها ويدخلان البيت)* أمي؟ أبي؟ *(يدخل الأب)* أهلا أبي. أبي، أقدم لك يوسف. يوسف، أقدم لك أبي *(يتصافحان)* أين أمي؟.
جورج	سوف ترجع بعد قليل. كان عليها أن تخرج.
ثيلما	ولكنها كانت تعرف أننا قادمان و-
جورج	لن تتأخر. زهور؟
يوسف	إنها للسيدة تشارلتون.
جورج	منذ زمن بعيد لم يشتر أحد لها زهورا. ضعها هنا. سوف تضعها في الماء عندما ترجع. هل ترغب في تناول شراب يا يوسف؟ خمر؟
ثيلما	المسلمون لا يشربون الخمر يا أبي.
جورج	دعيه يتكلم. فله لسان. يوسف؟
يوسف	شكرا لك. لا.
جورج	حسنا. سوف أتناول زجاجة من الخمر. إنها من "نيوكاسل". إنها نوع مشهور. هل سمعت عنه؟ *(يصب لنفسه كأسا).*
يوسف	نعم سمعت.
جورج	نوع قوي. شراب الرجال. يمكن أن تقول ذلك.
ثيلما	والدي يحب الشراب باعتدال.
جورج	إنها تخاف من أن أشرب كثيرا يا بني. إنني أفعل ذلك باعتدال. هل أنت متأكد من أنك لا ترغب في كأس؟
يوسف	لا – شكرا.
جورج	إنها خمر شهيرة في "تاينسايد". إنها وسيلة للاسترخاء مع الرجال.
ثيلما	مثلما قلت يا أبي. المسلمون لا يشربون.
جورج	نعم مثلما قلت. إذا ماذا تعمل؟
يوسف	عفوا!
جورج	لكي تسترخي، بعد يوم عمل. إذا كان هناك يوم عمل.
يوسف	اليمنيون يمضغون القات.

جورج	قطة؟ لقد سمعت عن أماكن فون يأكلون فيها الكلاب، ولكن القطط؟
يوسف	لا. لا سيد تشارلتون. أنت لا تفهمني. القات ورق شجر.
جورج	ورق شجر؟ أنت تقول إن اليمنيين يمضغون ورق الشجر — مثل القرود؟
الملثم	أين ي مي يا أبي؟
جورج	مثلما قلت، كان عليها أن تخرج. وكما قلت لن تتأخر. سوف تحضر شيئاً لنأكله، أنا متأكد من ذلك. ولن تحضر لحم خنزير *(يتناول الشراب)* إن هذا الشراب من أفضل ما ذقت في العالم. لقد اجتمعت أفضل العقول في هذا البلد لكي تصنعه. هيا يا بني، خذ بعضاً منه.
يوسف	هذا لطف شديد منك سيد تشارلتون، ولكن لا.
جورج	ماذا سيحدث لو أخذت بعضا منه. هل ستنزل صاعقة من السماء وتضربك؟
يوسف	الخمر محرّم.
جورج	نعم، حسنا. ماذا معك؟
يوسف	إنها نسخة من القرآن الكريم.
جورج	حسنا. ترى ما رأيك في هذا؟

(يحضر قاربه النموذجي).

يوسف	إنه مصنوع ببراعة.
جورج	لقد أمضيت الكثير من الوقت في صنعه. لدي وقت فراغ، يمكنك أن تقول ذلك.
الملثم	إن والدي بارع دائماً في الأعمال اليدوية، أليس كذلك يا أبي؟
جورج	لقد سمعت أن فتاك جيد في الملاكمة. هل هذا صحيح؟
يوسف	هذا لطف كبير منك.
جورج	لقد سمعت أنه هزم اثنين بالضربة القاضية. هل يمكنني أن ألقي نظرة على كتابك؟
يوسف	من الأفضل ألا تتناوله —
جورج	هيا يا بني. أريد أن ألقي نظرة فقط. لا ضرر في ذلك، أليس كذلك؟ أليس كذلك يا ثلم؟
الملثم	ربما يجدر بك أن تريه إياه يا يوسف.

(يناوله يوسف الكتاب ولكن بتردد).

جورج	لا أستطيع أن أفهمه.
يوسف	إنه مكتوب بالعربية.
جورج	آه العربية؟ إنه طلاسم بالنسبة إلي. فهل هذا الكتاب هو الحقيقة إذاً؟
يوسف	الحقيقة؟
جورج	أنت تعلم، أعني أنه إذا كان هذا الكتاب هو الحقيقة، فإن إنجيلنا لا يمكن أن يكون الحقيقة أيضا، أليس كذلك؟
يوسف	حسنا أنا —

33

جورج	وبالمثل، إذا كان إلهكم الله هو الإله الحقيقي، فإن إلهنا إذا ليس إلها حقيقيا، أليس كذلك؟
ثيلما	أبي، هل يمكن أن نترك هذا الموضوع؟
جورج	لا لا فوالدك شغوف بهذه الأشياء. إنني لست غبياً كما تظنين.
يوسف	بالنسبة للمسلمين، فإن القرآن هو الحقيقة.
جورج	بالنسبة للمسلمين – نعم. هل ترغب في تناول فنجان من الشاي؟
يوسف	سوف يكون ذلك لطيفا.
جورج	سوف تعد لك واحدا عندما ترجع. إذا – أنت تحب ابنتنا ثيلما.
يوسف	إنه أكثر من الحب.
جورج	أهكذا إذا؟
ثيلما	نحب بعضنا يا أبي.
جورج	الحب – نعم (يمسك بنموذج القارب) عليك أن تكون حريصاً وأنت تمسكه. إنه هش جدا ما ترى. إنه يبدو مثل القارب الحقيقي. ولكنه ليس كذلك. إنه محاكاة فقط.
يوسف	من فضلك سيد تشارلتون، هل يمكنني استعادة كتابي؟
جورج	أعطني دقيقة واحدة فقط؟ (يتفحصه) يجب أن تكون سعيدا. إنني أهتم بذلك. لدي إنجيل في مكان ما في البيت. ولكنني لا أهتم بالترتيل والأدعية التي لا أفهمها. هل تريد أن تتزوج ثيلما؟!
ثيلما	أبي!
جورج	إنه يبدو سؤالاً جيداً ومعقولا، حسنا؟
يوسف	أرغب في أن أقضي حياتي كلها معها، نعم.
جورج	ليس لديك زوجات أخريات في مكان آخر؟
ثيلما	هل يمكن أن تتوقف عن ذلك يا أبي؟
جورج	تعدد الزوجات، هذا ما يسمونه، أليس كذلك؟
ثيلما	لقد أرسلت أمي إلى الخارج، أليس كذلك؟
جورج	مثلما قلت، سوف تعود بعد دقيقة.
ثيلما	لقد أعددت لذلك، أيها اللعين.
جورج	هل تجرؤين على أن تنادي والدك بذلك؟
ثيلما	أنت لعين مخيف.
جورج	أهكذا الأمر، تضعين اللوم عليّ؟
يوسف	أرجوكما، أنا لا أفهم –
جورج	اهدأ يا بني. فأنت ضيف في هذا المنزل. كما إنك ضيف في هذا البلد. (يتناول مشروبه. يشرب كثيرا) لم لا تأخذ شرابا؟! إنه مهدئ جيد، أليس كذلك؟ ما الضرر في ذلك؟ هل ترغب في أخذ شربة صغيرة لعينة؟ إنه ليس سما، أتعرف ذلك؟ إنه خمر لعينة من "نيو كاسل". أترى يا فتى، عندما أشربها، فإن كل شيء يبدو أفضل. لا أشعر بأن لدي عرجاً في رجلي، وأستطيع أن أفكر في الذهاب إلى "ميل دام" في الصباح وربما

34

أحصل على بعض العمل. وأستطيع أن أفكر في أن هناك هدفاً أستيقظ من أجله في كل يوم، وأن إنجلترا ما زالت إنجلترا.

يوسف	آسف جدا من أجلك سيد تشارلتون.
جورج	آسف من أجلي؟ أنت؟ عربي؟ آسف من أجلي؟
يوسف	ربما علينا الذهاب يا ثيلما. لا أشعر بارتياح هنا. هل يمكنني استعادة نسختي من القرآن هنا يا سيد تشارلتون؟
جورج	عربي وقح – آسف من أجلي!
يوسف	القرآن الكريم من فضلك *(يذهب ليأخذه. لا يسمح له الأب).*
ثيلما	والدي، أعطه القرآن.
جورج	اه،انا الآن أتلقى الأوامر من ابنتي، أليس كذلك؟
يوسف	أرجوك يا سيد تشارلتون. أنا لا أريد أي مشاكل.
جورج	آه أتسمعين ذلك؟ العربي لا يريد أي مشاكل. إنه يريد أن يأتي إلى هنا ويسرق وظائفنا ويغري نساءنا ويهزأ بالكثير منا، ولكنه لا يريد أي مشاكل.
يوسف	أرجوك. أعطني القرآن، سوف أذهب الآن.
جورج	لا شك أنك تحسب أنني غبي يا بني. وكأنني لا أعرف ما يحدث. فأنا كنت أحارب من أجل بلدي، ثم أرجع إلى وطني ولا أجد عملاً وأجد المكان مليئا بالغرباء. يا له من عود لطيف إلى الوطن، نعم؟ ومن المفروض أن أرحب بك إلى هذا المنزل، أليس كذلك؟ وأن أتمنى لك الأمنيات السعيدة مع ابنتي، ويداك السوداوان القذرتان تستوليان عليها و–
ثيلما	توقف عن هذا يا أبي!
جورج	أتوقف؟ هو وغيره من العرب غير الشرعيين هم الذين يحتاجون من يوقفهم. قطعوا نصف الكرة الأرضية، ليسرقوا وظائفنا، وهاأنا ذا وقد ولدت على بعد بضع شوارع من "ميل دام"، لا أستطيع العمل. هل تعرف معنى ذلك يا بني، رجل بدون عمل؟
ثيلما	أنت تفعل ما بوسعك يا أبي.
جورج	أنا لم أفعل شيئاً. أنا بلا فائدة. وهو من جعلني بلا فائدة. سأجبر كل واحد منهم على مغادرة شيلدز، سأعيدهم إلى أكواخهم الطينية اللعينة أو إلى أي مكان ينتمون إليه، لأن هذا ليس مكانهم.
يوسف	الكتاب من فضلك، سأذهب.
جورج	أهذا كل ما يزعجك، كتابك ؟ ولا يعنيك أي حياة هدمتها؟ حسناً هذا رأيي في كتابك *(يذهب ليقطع القرآن إلى نصفين. يلتقط يوسف نموذج القارب ليتلفه. ابتعدا عن بعضهما)* أتلف هذا القارب، وستصبح من الأموات.
يوسف	لا أريد سوى القرآن. وسأذهب بعدها.
جورج	هذه هي طبيعتك الحقيقية؟ تأخذ وظائفنا وبناتنا ثم تتلف الشيء الوحيد الذي تركه الإنسان. أترين ذلك يا ثيلما؟
ثيلما	أرجوك ضع الكتاب يا أبي.
جورج	اجعليه يبعد يديه العربية القذرة عن هذا القارب.
ثيلما	يوسف؟

35

(بعد الابتعاد، يدفع الأب يوسف، لكنه من الواضح أنه لا يقدر على العراك. تدخل مارجريت أثناء المشاجرة).

مارجريت	ما الـ ـ
ثيلما	أوقفيهما يا أمي! *(تبعدهما عن بعضهما. يدمر القارب في هذه الأثناء)* أمي، أقدم لك يوسف.
يوسف	*(يلتقط باقة الزهور)* لقد جلبت لك بعض الزهور يا سيدة تشارلتون.
مارجريت	يا إلهي.
يوسف	يجب أن تضعيها في الماء وإلا ستموت.
ثيلما	لقد تعمد إبعادك يا أمي. أراد أن يحسم القضية مع يوسف.
جورج	إنه لا يزال منزلي اللعين *(يفتح زجاجة خمر. كان على وشك أن يشرب حينما أخذها يوسف منه ليشربها).*
يوسف	أهكذا أصبحت رجلا يا سيد تشارلتون؟ *(ينتزع الأب الزجاجة)* ليس من أجلك، إنه من أجل ثيلما.
جورج	لا أريد أن أسمعك تنادي باسم ابنتي أيها العربي الشريد. أريدك أن تخرج من هذا المنزل إلى الأبد، ولن أجعلها هي الأخرى تنطق باسمك أبدا.
ثيلما	لا يمكنك أن تفعل ذلك يا أبي، أنا ــ
جورج	هل هذا واضح لكما؟ ــ
يوسف	ليس كل البيض مثلك.
جورج	ماذا؟!
يوسف	ليس جميعهم يمتلئون بالكراهية *(يحاول الأب الذهاب إليه مجددا. تمسك به مارجريت وثيلما).*
جورج	اخرج! اخرج!
مارجريت	أرجوك، اذهب يا بني.
يوسف	آسف يا سيدة تشارلتون، أنا ــ
مارجريت	هل يمكن أن تذهب فقط؟ *(يخرج يوسف. يضعان الأب على الكرسي).*
جورج	إلى ماذا تنظرين إذًا؟
مارجريت	إنني أنظر إليك.
جورج	انتهي بالشاي يا امرأة! هل أصبحت بالصمم أم ماذا؟! *(إلى ثيلما)* ثم هل تقفين هنا لتنظري إليّ بدهشة مثل الأخرق اللعين؟
ثيلما	هل ستقولين أي شيء يا أمي؟
جورج	لماذا بحق السماء ستقول أي شيء؟
ثيلما	لن تقولي شيئا، أليس كذلك؟
جورج	ليس لديها شيء لتقوله. هل لديك يا امرأة؟
مارجريت	في الحقيقية، لدي شيء لأقوله.
ثيلما	تكلمي إذًا. أريد أن أسمع ما ستقولين. أردت دائما أن أسمعه.
جورج	ما هو إذًا؟ هذا "الشيء" الذي لديك لتقوليه؟

36

مارجريت	ــ أنا
جورج	تكلمي وقولي هذا الشيء اللعين، ثم أكملي صنع الشاي!
مارجريت	شعوري بالأسف حيالك على مدى هذه السنوات.
جورج	ماذا؟
مارجريت	أنا لا أقول شيئًا. أنا أشمئز من نفسي كما أشمئز منك تمامًا.
جورج	اللعنة، ماذا تقولين؟!
مارجريت	ليس خطأك، أليس كذلك؟
جورج	هذا يكفي *(يضربها).*
مارجريت	*(في نهاية الأمر)* تضع اللوم على الحرب، والعرب، وأي شيء آخر، إلا نفسك! وماذا عنا إذًا؟ هذه العائلة. أنا وأنت وثيلما. لقد كنت ضعيفة وتافهة، لقد اعتدت على أن أحتفظ بهدوني عندما يكون من المستحيل ذلك.
جورج	إذا أنت تتحازين للعرب الآن يا امرأة؟ لقد أتوا إلى هنا ليأخذوا وظائفنا و—
مارجريت	بالطبع — كل شيء هو خطأ يوسف. الإحباط والبطالة والفقر، ترجع كلها إلى هذا الرجل اليمني الصغير، أليس كذلك؟
جورج	لماذا أتيها اللعينة؟ — *(يذهب إليها مهدداً لكنه يكسر القارب. يدخل البائع بالصحف).*
بائع الصحف	عدد خاص! اقرأ كل شيء! اقرأ عن اتحاد كرة القدم المبارة النهائية في "هورسلي هيل" اليوم! إنه الوداع للساحليين! عدد خاص! عدد خاص! *(إلى ثيلما)* هل أنت بخير؟
ثيلما	بخير؟
بائع الصحف	هذه الأزهار *تذبل (يفعل شيئاً ما بالأزهار. يبيع صحيفة للأب. يقود ثيلما والأم إلى خارج المسرح. يقول الجملة الأخيرة للأب قبل أن يقوده إلى الخارج هو الآخر)* هل تعرف أن المباراة النهائية سوف تكون أمام "أكرينجتون ستانلي". *(بائع الصحف وحده على المسرح. يوسف يندفع إلى الخلف في حالة هياج).*
بائع الصحف	توقف! توقف! أين الحريق؟
يوسف	ماذا؟!
بائع الصحف	هذه ليست نهاية العالم.
يوسف	ماذا تعرف؟
بائع الصحف	هل تعني، بغض النظر عن كل شيء؟
	(يوسف يذهب إلى نُزل العمال ليقابله علي. يُتبع بمشهد عربي).
علي	يوسف — ماذا حدث؟
يوسف	لا شيء.
علي	هناك شيء غير مطمئن. تعال إلى هنا. *(يشم نفسه)* لقد شربت. هذا سيئ جدا بالنسبة إلى المسلم. أين كنت *(يوسف لا يرد)* أهذا ما يحدث عندما تذهب إلى بيت المرأة البيضاء؟
يوسف	اسمها ثيلما.

37

علي	كنت في البداية تلعب مباريات الملاكمة. واليوم تشرب. وزملاؤك البحارة يكادون يموتون من الجوع.
يوسف	ماذا؟
علي	نحن لا نعرف ماذا نفعل يا يوسف. لقد انضممنا إلى حركة البحارة الأقلية. ووافقنا على مقاطعة السفن. لقد قالوا أن هذا سيحقق العدل.
يوسف	عدل؟
علي	بالطبع، أنت لا تفهم. لقد شربت الخمر. لا يمكن أن تكون على ما يرام. عليك أن تغادر النزل الآن.
يوسف	أغادر؟
علي	لدي ما هو أهم منك لأفكر فيه. اذهب.

(يخرج يوسف. يذهب مباشرة إلى شارب).

يوسف	أنا جاهز.
شارب	نعم، يبدو عليك ذلك يا بني.
يوسف	أين الرجل الذي ألاكمه؟
شارب	هاهو (حشد يتجمع للقتال. يوسف قاس ويهزم الرجل بسهولة. شارب يتدخل) يكفي هذا يا يوسف. لقد هزمت الرجل تماما.
يوسف	أين التالي؟
شارب	أنت مطرقة مقبنة، أليس كذلك؟ كل شيء له وقت يا بني. كل شيء له وقت (بصوت عالٍ) أي منافسين لمطرقة مقبنة؟

(لا يزال يوسف يتظاهر بالملاكمة. تدخل ثيلما).

ثيلما	يوسف!
يوسف	نعم.
ثيلما	أنا آسفة يا يوسف.
يوسف	أنا آسف أيضاً.
ثيلما	لم أكن أريد أن يحدث شيء من هذا.
يوسف	أنا أعرف. سوف ألاكم الآن.
ثيلما	هل هذه هي الإجابة؟
يوسف	وحده الله الذي يعرف الإجابات. لكنني ألاكم.
ثيلما	أنا اسمع أن الأشياء ساءت أحوالها بالنسبة لليمنيين.
يوسف	يجب أن أكون جاهزا للمباراة التالية.
ثيلما	لماذا لا نذهب إلى السينما؟ ونشاهد فيلم "*الباحثون عن الذهب في برودواي*"، في سينما جراند إلكتريك. وهناك فيلم ملوّن كذلك.
يوسف	ليس لدي أي وقت، آسف.
ثيلما	يوسف، أنا أحبك.
يوسف	نعم، أعرف ذلك.
ثيلما	ربما يكون هذا ديني، أليس كذلك؟

38

يوسف	دينك؟
الملثم	أنت والإسلام. ربما يكون ديني هو الحب. لنا ملك. إنه لنا. لا كتاب، لا نبي، لكن – *(يتعانقان).*
بارب	حسنًا يا يوسف. لقد حان الوقت *(ندخل في مبارة أخرى. مرة أخرى، يقضي يوسف على منافسه بقسوة)* كما لو كان الشيطان بداخلك يا يوسف. مطرقة مقنبة، أليس كذلك؟ من يستطيع هزيمته؟
يوسف	لا أحد يستطيع هزيمتي *(يحصل على الجائزة المالية).*
الملثم	يوسف، أنا خائنة.
يوسف	خائنة.
الملثم	عليك وعلى نفسي. ما الذي يحدث؟
يوسف	لقد رأيت الرجال البيض في الحلبة. وهم لا يستطيعون هزيمتي. أنا اليمني العربي. الشخص الأدنى. إنهم ليسوا أقوياء بما يكفي لهزيمتي. ربما يكون أبوك على حق. ربما لا يصلح أن نختلط إلا في هذه الحلبة.
الملثم	يجب ألا تصدق ذلك.
يوسف	لم لا؟ إنه من يبقى واقفًا في الحلبة.
	(الآن ربما يفوز يوسف بمزيد من المباريات بأسلوبه الخاص. يتظاهر بالملاكمة في طريقه خارجًا من المسرح. يدخل تشارترز مرتديًا منشفة ومستعدًا للتدليك).
تشارترز	والآن أين هذا المدلّك اللعين؟ *(يدخل بائع الصحف ويغير مظهره بسرعة).*
بائع الصحف	هنا يا سيدي! *(تشارترز يستلقى لتدليكه).*
تشارترز	تأكد من أنك قد دفعت زيت التدليك هذا يا فتى.
بائع الصحف	إنه دافئ تمامًا يا سيدي!
تشارترز	أريد تدليكًا جيدًا وليس لكزات. تظن زوجتي أن لدي بعض الوزن الزائد.
بائع الصحف	أنت تعني يا سيدي، أن حبيبتك ليست مبتهجة تمامًا بشكلك الذي يشبه شكل أدونيس؟
تشارترز	*(ينظر إليه عن قرب)* هل عملت قبل ذلك نادلًا؟
بائع الصحف	أنا يا سيدي! ما هذا الكلام!
تشارترز	ماذا عن عملك كمصفف شعر أو حلاق؟
بائع الصحف	أنا لا أعرف الفرق بين مقص الشعر وماكينة قص العشب يا سيدي!
تشارترز	حانوتي؟
بائع الصحف	حانوتي!
تشارترز	هل هذا إليس؟ *(يدخل إليس).*
إليس	أنا هنا.
تشارترز	أخبرني بآخر الأحداث يا إليس.
إليس	البحارة العرب يقاطعون السفن في ساوث شيلدز.

تشارتر	والبحارة البيض؟
إليس	لا يزالون ملتزمين تقريبًا، رغم الضغط الذي يتعرضون له من قبل حركة الأقلية.
تشارتر	لقد فهمت.
إليس	إنهم يدعون إلى اجتماع كبير من أجل التضامن.
تشارتر	من واقع خبرتي، فإنني أرى أن التضامن لا يساوي شيئًا، إذا لم تكن له قوة تحميه.
إليس	لن يكون نظام العمل الجديد اذ فائدة.
تشارتر	لقد صدّق اتحادك عليه. وهذا له تأثير في "أنتويرب".
إليس	يراودني فقط من القلق ما سيد تشارترز يا. إنه إجراء مثير للخلاف.
تشارتر	يُطبق نظام العمل على جميع البحارة بصرف النظر عن الجنسية أو اللون.
إليس	الأفضلية تكون لمن بقي دون عمل لفترات أطول، مما يعني أن تكون الأفضلية للبحارة البيض.
تشارتر	هل تريد يا إليس إنك تنتقد علنًا هذا النظام الجديد، الذي قُدم بعد تعاونك الكامل، وبعد مناقشات طويلة وصريحة مع الاتحاد؟
إليس	إنه فقط يحتاج إلى وقت للتفكير مرة أخرى ـ
تشارتر	أحتاج فقط إلى معرفة ما إذا كان اتحاد السفن يمكنه الاعتماد على تعاونك، وعلى توصيات الخبراء، كما كان يحدث في الماضي، من أجل التحسين الشامل لهذه الصناعة كهدف. في الواقع يا إليس، أريد أن أسأل هل نحن متفقان أم مختلفان هنا؟
إليس	حسنًا، أنا ـ
تشارتر	لهذا أهمية حيوية جدا قبل أن نبدأ فيما هو أبعد من ذلك.
إليس	أستطيع أن أرى مشكلات كبيرة تلوح في الأفق.
تشارتر	أين تقف يا رجل؟ مع نظام العمل هذا؟ حسنا؟
إليس	سوف يقدم الاتحاد الوطني للبحارة الدعم الكامل لنظام العمل. في "هُل"، و"كارديف"، و"ساوث شيلدز ".
تشارتر	أنت رجل صالح يا إليس. (إلى بائع الصحف) اللعنة ـ بالهداوة يا فتى! إن جسدي ليس قطعة من المعجون تقوم بلكمها!
بائع الصحف	راحتك التامة هي هدفي يا سيدي.
تشارتر	أنت تتحدث فقط ولا تعمل شيئا. والآن لا يجب أن يظهر عليك أنك منزعج يا إليس. لا يفهم الناس الضغط الذي يقع علينا. تسيير أساطيل كبيرة من السفن عندما يكون الاقتصاد العالمي على وشك الانهيار. انظر إلى أمريكا. تعاني من مشكلات ضخمة تعيق الاقتصاد. والجميع يعتقدون أنه يمكنهم الوصول إلى أي مكان والحصول على وظيفة بصرف النظر عن المكان الذي يأتون منه. مثل الأطفال في العربة ينتظرون الحلوى. حسنًا، الكثير من الحلوى قد تضر الأطفال. يا إلهي! هل أنت شخص مضطرب لعين؟ هذا يكفي بالنسبة لي. (يتكلم بوقاحة وينصرف غاضبًا).
بائع الصحف	(يجري تعديلًا سريعًا) جريدة يا سيد إليس؟
إليس	ماذا؟

40

بائع الصحف	إنجلترا. تيتز جازيديشن" من اليوم عدد يشتري أن بربرترا اخبرأنك فكرت 101. برقم 4 رقم تستبدل "فاكسرافير" الآيا أستر أمام للبطولة من ج تخرج ميل في 20 سرعة تحدداء تلغاء – توقع جديد مروري طريق قانون توقع أننا رغم ر لليمل سقطت. (الجريدة السير يشتري). شيء لكل اقرأ. الساعة ؟كلذلك سيليا ،ونيونيو شهر في
إليس	معن (جبرخي).
	(تيت. جرر مارمدتخدة الجريدة جروج أرأ)
مارجريت	أن يريدني ماذا استممت. هذا قيلا. لا ءشي أي. جروج يا يا ئانئا شلق منى تدرأ إذا لكن ،كذلك يكن لم ماربوا ،صحيحاً قلتها ما مأربا؟لعلها في ما لكل هذا. معمي تحدثتك ذلك كان إذا فأفعله ،اعتذارا الا ج. روج آسفة أنا ،رمر الأمر
	(هبراق جنموذنصصحف لتيتمامها أمر ميرو جروج ضهبني).
	(الرجل يوقع. مبارة بكل ليفوز الخاص أسلوبه ويطبق ،يقاتل يوسف) تات المباري متعهد لتخد منتصر وهو. شارب يلاحظها أضا. الأخير (يرياه.
هاري	ب. شارب يا ءشي لكل هذا ،ننصح
شارب	؟ينعتي اذام
هاري	ه. تدعدوا امتلمنئبيقة مطرقة، يبرالع كاتف أقصد
شارب	؟هنع اذام
هاري	الملامكة. من مزيد لا
شارب	؟هذا يهينع أن ضرتفترا من الذي ام
هاري	مع الحاضر في شيلديدز في التوتر من الكثير هناك. ما سمعت ما أعني سوءا. تاراراتلتوا هذه يزيديد وهو. بالعر
شارب	؟رسخي ماداموا بالعرم كلالمالا وجود عنائمتا أنك تعني هل
هاري	في يتيببون الآن. ننانا. نظافننا ليأخذوا هنا يأتون إنهم. لولان دور ما هذا حلبة في المالية الجايزنة كل نونيأخذو. يعيصناب راطاضتضا ثوث الملامكة.
شارب	؟نالآ اذامو
هاري	بي. العرا الفتى أمام المتباريين نيين من مزيد كناه نونيك لن
	(هاري. جيخرج. بهذه يخبره يوسف إلى شارب بهب يذ) عن المعلومات تامه. المباراة بطءب ويبهدأ ،بالملامكة رهظتيتن يوسف. الإشارة طريق (امليه. لتخد شارب يخرج. شارب
ثمليا	أنه يملع (التوقف من القليل). يوسف يا للمقاتلة طريقة أكثر يوجد أجل من بر تحارا أن هو الإثات لطريقة فضلأو. ذاتك ليكع الإجابة، الله ولدى الله هوللقيا ما هذا. نفسك أجل من فقط وليس ،نالآخري (نانافقيعصلا) بك. مؤمنة وأنا ،كذلكلآ،
ترمديون	اليوم، المنصة على معي ،يلاني؟زم (الحشم على بةطخ يلقي لليدخ) ا ايعويبستس لم إنهم. مقبنة بمبمطرقة منكم الكثير يعرفه ،قرشيش الله عبد يوسف فسيو. أخ يا يا لك الكلمة. المالية. أسمارا هم تهزهز نلو ،مكلاكم متهزه

<hr>

41

| يوسف | لم يعد لدينا ما نخسره. يجب أن نكون عاقدين العزم. لقد أتيت إلى هذا البلد من أجل حياة جديدة. وقريبًا لن يكون للعرب في هذا البلد حياة *(ثيلما وجورج ومارجريت يتابعون ما يحدث)*. |
| تريمدون | إن يوسف يقول الحقيقة يا زملائي. لدينا عدو مشترك. إنها الرأسمالية البريطانية، وحكومة حزب العمال. وتمامًا كما يتهمون العرب هنا، فإن الرأسمالية وحكومة حزب العمال يبعثان بسفن أسلحة ضد العرب في مصر، مثلما يبعثان طائرات لتقصف العرب في فلسطين. نحن ندعوا البحارة أيًا كانت جنسيتهم إلى الاجتماع في "ميل دام" لعمل مسيرة. انضموا إلى حركة البحارة الأقلية، انضموا إلى الحزب الشيوعي. اهزموا مُلاك السفن، واليبي سي 5 ونظام العمل. الأبيض والأسود – اتحدوا وحاربوا! |

(يدخل تشارترز المسرح ويرفقه إليس).

تشارترز	هل تعتقد يا إليس أنه يعير اهتمامًا لهؤلاء البحارة العرب؟ إنه يريد إسقاط الحكومة بأي ثمن. لذلك فإنه إذا اعتقد أن هذه الحركة ستثير ما يكفي من المشاكل، فسيكون هناك ليدير حملة ويثير هياجًا مضاعفًا. إنها كلمة من السلطات العليا هي ما يحتاجه هؤلاء المهيجون ليتوقفوا. هل قمت بإعداد القليل من رجال الاتحاد الوطني من البحارة الصالحين؟
إليس	سيكونون مستعدين عند الحاجة.
تشارترز	سوف نحتاجهم على حسب ما أرى من سير الأحداث. انظر إلى هؤلاء العرب؟ إنهم فقط يبحثون عن المشاكل. إن بحوزتهم سكاكين وأرجل كراسي وحجارة رصيف. وهذا العربي ذو الصوت العالي هناك، ليست له فائدة. تأكد من الإمساك به.
يوسف	لقد طلبت من جميع زملائي العرب الثبات على العزم. لا تقبلوا الانضمام.
تشارترز	إذا كانوا يريدون المشاكل، فسيحصلون عليها. الشرطة مستعدة.
تريمدون	لقد أدى الأخ يوسف أداءً رائعًا! إن العرب نسبتهم 100%! لم ينضم واحد منهم. إنهم يقفون صفًا واحدًا! إن القرار لكم الآن أيها البحارة البيض. تماسكوا! يجب أن تكون ساوث شيلدز هي مركز الإزعاج. كل الموانئ الأخرى تنظر إليكم كمثال يحتذى. تماسكوا!
تشارترز	تأكد من أن بحارتك يخترقون الطوق عند الإشارة يا إليس.
إليس	يبدو ذلك قبيحا للغاية.
تشارترز	للمرء كل الحق في الحصول على العمل في بلده. لا يمكن حرماننا من ذلك. أريد من رجالك أن يتخطوا الخطوط ويقتحموا مكاتب لجنة التجارة.
إليس	سيفنيم الوضع.
تشارترز	هذا ما يحدث للبراكين. أليس كذلك. اذهبوا!

(يقتحم الرجال ويندلع الشغب. تجنب يوسف الاعتقال بسبب مهارته. لقد كان هناك رجل مطعون. يعتمد مدى الشغب على الأعداد المتوافرة والموارد).

| تشارترز | أحضروا هذا العربي المشاغب اللعين! *(إخفاق في الوصول إلى يوسف. ينحسر الشغب. يمشي بائع الصحف بين الحطام).* |
| بائع الصحف | اعتقالات واسعة في "ميل دام"! قُبض على واحد وعشرين من العرب وخمسة من أعضاء حركة البحارة الأقلية. طُعن شرطي واحد. *(ثيلما تبحث عن يوسف. في النهاية تجده وتعانقه).* |

الميلا	احضني فقط يا يوسف.
يوسف	كان الوضع سيئًا جدًا بالنسبة لنا يا ثيلما.
الميلا	على الأقل أنت حر. ما الذى سيحدث للآخرين؟

(موسيقى إسلامية. دخل بحارة يمنيون ووقفوا للصلاة. فى حين كانت الأسماء التالية تُقرأ، وموزع الصحف يتحرك بين الرجال، ويربت على أكتافهم وهم يتركون خشبة المسرح. يقرأ من جريدة جازيت).

بائع الصحف	السيد على سعيد، حُكم عليه بستة عشر شهرا مع الأشغال الشاقة والترحيل. على صالح 12 شهراً أشغالاً شاقة وترحيل.
يوسف	لقد سُحقت المقاومة العربية. لم تعد هناك حركة البحارة الأقلية.
بائع الصحف	ثابت محمود، ستة أشهر أشغالا شاقة وترحيل. محمد يوسف ستة أشهر أشغالا شاقة وترحيل.
الميلا	وماذا عن نُزل العمال؟
يوسف	أغلق يا ثيلما. كيف يمكن للسيد حسن حسن تحمل إدارته؟
بائع الصحف	صالح أحمد، أربعة أشهر أشغالا شاقة وترحيل، عبد الله على، ثمانية أشهر أشغالا شاقة وترحيل.
الميلا	أحضرت لك بعض الطعام.
يوسف	شكرا لك *(يضعه أرضا)* كان الله فى عوننا.
الميلا	سيحل الشتاء قريبا. علينا مساعدتك.
بائع الصحف	عبد الله المعيال، 12 شهرا أشغالا شاقة. عبد الله محمد، أربعة أشهر وترحيل.
الميلا	ليس لديك شيء. يجب أن تقدم طلبًا للجنة المعونة العامة للإعانة الخارجية. هذا بلد متحضر.
بائع الصحف	أيها الموظف – استمارة طلب!

(بائع الصحف يتقدم إلى الموظف على المكتب).

الموظف	*(يختم الطلب)* الطلب مرفوض.
بائع الصحف	على عنون، 8 أشهر أشغالا شاقة وترحيل. عبد الله زيد، أربعة أشهر أشغالا شاقة وترحيل.
الميلا	ماذا سنفعل يا يوسف؟
يوسف	على نُزل العمال تقديم التماس للاتحاد الوطني *(يدخل على ليقرأ خطاب للاتحاد. الجزء الأخير من الخطاب يقرأه إليس بصوت عالٍ أثناء دخوله).*
على	"السادة الأعزاء، لا نرى شيئًا سوى مجاعة تتجه نحونا، حيث إننا ككثير من المدانين ليس لدينا ما نأكله وكل هذا بسبب اتحادنا ...... *(يدخل إليس).*
إليس	... كلنا نطالبكم ونأمل ونتضرع إلى الله أن تجيبوا التماسنا. " لا يمكنني إيصال هذه الرسالة. سأسلمها إلى مكتب المستعمرات.
بائع الصحف	سالم غالب، 12 شهرا أشغالا شاقة وترحيل *(يدخل مسؤول وزارة الخارجية لأخذ الرسالة).*
مسؤول الخارجية	اكتبي رسالة آنسة بريسم *(يمشى أثناء الإملاء)*. "أعتقد أن مسألة الديون التي على البحارة العرب، أمر يخص البحارة أنفسهم، ويخص المسؤولين

قول أما عن اللزل الخاصة بهم، الذين اعتقد أنهم يتصرفون نيابة عنهم. قول
إن البطالة بين العرب بسبب نظام العمل الجديد، فهو باطل تمامًا. هل
يمكنك تهجي كلمة "باطل" آنسة بريسم؟ جيد ـ تؤثر البطالة على كل من
البحارة البريطانيين والعرب و هي بسبب الكساد العام" – لكل من البحارة
العرب والبريطانيين يعانون من البطالة بالطبع. يكفى هذا يا آنسة بريسم.

فحصلا عناب	إبرا هيم أحمد 12 شهرا الأشغالا شاقة وترحيل.
ثملي	لا يستطيع العيش هكذا يا أمى. لا يجدر بأى شخص العيش هكذا.
ماجريت	اذا ماذا يمكن أن نفعل يا ثمليا؟
ثملي	يمكنك أن تطلبى من أبى أن يستاضافته.
ماجريت	استضافته؟ في منزلنا؟
ثملي	إليه. ان كان مكان و لا مال و لا سيد لديه منزل ليس إليه.
ماجريت	لم يتحدث أبوك معى بكلمة واحدة منذ ذلك اليوم.
ثملي	اعاميجم بنا ذلك فعله الذى ما ظرنا انا أنا. و لا
ماجريت	أنت تطتطبين المعجزات يا عزيزتي.
فحصلا عناب	عبد المجيد 4 أشهر الأشغالا شاقة وترحيل.
ثملي	علهله. لابد أن هناك ما نكمننا أن دلا.
تشارترز	فعله. هناك داءما ءشيء يمكننا أن نكان هنا.
ثملي	ماذا تعنى؟
تشارترز	ذلك الفتى العربي المعجبة به. ـ يمكنه تقديم طلب للحصول على إعانة داخلية. في معهد "هارتون".
ثملي	لَم تخبرني بهذا؟
تشارترز	أشار وفر وطعامًا وأوى مأوى سيجيد أصحابه وأو هو.
ثملي	معهد هارتون – إصلاحية؟ شيءلدليز؟
تشارترز	ماذا في الاسم؟ طاب يومكم.
فحصلا عناب	عبدالله محمود، أربعة أشهر أشغالا شاقة وترحيل. سعيد سعد، ستّة أشهر أشغالا شاقة وترحيل.

(يخديا لخسفو يويب للاطلاع على قائمة اليمنيين المبعدين).

	محمد أحمد 15 شهرا الأشغالا شاقة. عبد الله صالح حلج 12 شهرا الأشغالا شاقة وترحيل.
ثملي	يوسف خذ هذا. اذا. للألأف فإنها آخر جنيهات معي.
فسو	لا يمكنني نني أخذ المزيد منك يا ثمليا. ليس اذا هذا خطأك.
ثملي	كل لك أملكه ملك وما فسو، ك أحبك يا أنا
فسو	شيئا أملك لا كلك لكك ليكون أملكه الذى وما.
ثملي	ماذا عن معهد هارتون؟
فسو	قناريزرز سوف الله إن نقول بلادى، فى
ثملي	فكر جيدا يا يوسف. على الأقل هارتون قد تعطيك – شيئا.

44

يوسف	معِ أسأحاول
	(بنائع الصفحتبث حتيدحث مع الموظف على مكتبه الذي يأتي إليه وباتي يه مسرعا.)
الموظف	حسنا حسن يوسف عبد الله قرشي؟
يوسف	معن
الموظف	هل ترغب فى تقديم طلب للإعانة الداخلية فى معهد هاورتون؟
يوسف	لا أرى، ولكن سأفعل.
الموظف	من فضلك، بنعم أجك، أو لا .ً
يوسف	معن
الموظف	وتوافق على الالتزام بالشروط التي تنطبق على مثل قبيطت هذا الطلب؟
يوسف	لا أعرف عن من هذه مثل الأشياء
الموظف	لا .ً أو بنعم تجيب أن يجب ثانية تذكيرك تود أو.
يوسف	معن
الموظف	كان كبلطك أن أخبرك فى رغب أر (جزنونم من النماء جزء متعخبيت) اداج ديد جاجهان مسم موسوح الآن للسكن والمعيشة فى معهد هاورتون، وكذلك يمكنكين القول بأن هناك اددا كبيرا من مواطناطكنين أيضا .ً
يوسف	شكرا لك.
ثليم	أفضل من لا شيء يا يوسف فى الوقت تقت الحالي.
الموظف	يتضمن الطلب على مثل هذا الطرووطرط التي تقببط على افقت وافق على الالتزام بالشروط .الطلب، هذا مقدم بطلب للإعانة الداخلية خلال 12 شهر أو أى أجنبي أى تقديم الالتزام ما يتبنى من هذا البلد هذا دخوله من للترحيل بتبيلسميم نفسه البلد.
يوسف	اذام؟
الموظف	هو كما بنجنبأكعدك وضعخذؤى، يانيانة البريطاهناط الموبايان فى هو كما.
بانع الصحفت	لقد أتى من دعو ندن، وعدن من هذه اله جهعلطيريبرب انيانا!
تشارترتز	من ندعن؟ مطرق مقة بنبنة؟
الموظف	الآن نأشأنأنك قد صدر أمر الترحيل علاميالك إبى واجب من.
يوسف	مهم- أفثدحى الذا ما؟ لا
الموظف	دلابلا ج خاروخ شيليدز ج جار كللك تقنت تريتت متتس.
ثليم	لكن لا يمكنك فعل هذا- اذا. (تعاضرار الموظف.)
الموظف	من فضلك، لا تعتتد يدينى على موظف حكوم محلى .يمكمك. طاب يو باب. (يخرج. بيد لخلش شرط.)
الشرطي	قف هنا يا بني .ينب يبقى الزنزنانا فى حتى ترت لحل.
	(ريفر يوسف عندما يحاول الشرطي اعتقاله. تتبعه صافرة الشرطي. لاحقا، رأت العائلة يأكلملها ها وسفوي، وهو يتيبدرفرده وحدايا).
ثليم	إذا سترتاء فى الخارج مثل الطرجل الرجل أبى يا إذا الطريدوا الحيوان مثل الخارج فى ستترئتر إذا الذى الوحيد الرجل الرجل تمامات، أما ألا ترى ذلك؟ذلكلك يتخلخصين نونون من كليكما عندك ناساني بسباب مامداكلك يا وطنهنا!" أو آأفعن معم،أنت أنتت تقوم بعبسمهلهمله القذار يا مضهراغأ. "أرسل العربرى إلى

45

أبى، لم لا؟ وما فائدة ذلك لك ولأمى الآن؟ وما فائدة ذلك لنا كلنا؟ لكنك تستمر فيه يا أبى. إنك تقوم بعملك جيدا.

جورج	**(بعد صمت)** أدخلي الفتى. **(يدخل يوسف. وتدخل الأم. يوقفها جورج)** أتوقع فنجان الشاى فى وقته المعتاد.

(تشارترز وإليس يشربان في نادي إليس الخاص، وبائع الصحف هو النادل).

تشارترز	أنت جديد بالنادي، ألست كذلك أيها النادل؟
بائع الصحف	جديد جدا يا سيدى.
تشارترز	منذ متى وأنت هنا بالضبط؟
بائع الصحف	منذ دقيقتين تقريبا.
تشارترز	أعطني "جى و تى"، ومن الأفضل مضاعفتها. ماذا ستتناول يا إليس؟
إليس	أفضل الالتزام بنصف كأس من الخمر.
تشارترز	ولاؤك لجذورك من الطبقة العاملة، أليس كذلك؟
إليس	لا أدري ما أفعله فى مثل هذا النادى!
تشارترز	لا تحصل على ملابس جلد أحمر مثل هذا فى "بويليرميكيرس أرمرز"، أليس كذلك؟ تبدو مضطرباً يا إليس.
إليس	الحالة مريعة لعرب ساوث شيلد.
تشارترز	جاءوا إلى هذه البلاد للعمل. وأضربوا وسببوا عنفاً وفوضى، أعني -
إليس	نعم، أعرف، لكن -
بائع الصحف	هل يمكن أن أتجرأ وأقول شيئا يا سيد إليس، سيدى؟
إليس	ماذا؟!
بائع الصحف	أعرف أنه ليس من شأنى، وربما لا يكون كلامى مرتبا، ولكن-
إليس	حسنا، ما الذى أردت قوله؟ قل ما تريد!
بائع الصحف	فقط أن – حسنا، سيد تشارترز يحتقرك.
إليس	ماذا؟!
تشارترز	دائماً ما كنت أفعل. لم أكن أحترمك على الإطلاق.
إليس	لماذا كل ذلك؟
تشارترز	النادل أذكى مما يبدو. لا يقول الكثير.
إليس	ما الذى يجري هنا يا سيد تشارترز؟
تشارترز	ليس الكثير. غير أنك عار على اتحادك ودائما ما كنت كذلك. لا عجب أنهم تخلصوا منك.
إليس	لكني حاولت دائماً التعاون مع اتحاد الشحن و-
تشارترز	ليس عملك أن تتعاون معنا يا بنى. إن عملك أن تقوم بالتضييق علينا بقوة لصالح أعضائك. تماما كما نضيق عليك نحن.
إليس	تعرف أنني لم أؤمن ابدا بالمواجهة!

46

تشارترز	ما لذنب البحر. لتُحقق لي يا بني. هذا إذا؟ هذه الوظيفة التي تقنعها الذي ما تشارترز تتبات التربة؟ أتعرف؟ أقا. حق شيء هنا إنه فيقا تحت أوّل إنسان. وسو في تمامًا.
إليس	لكني قدمت لك المساعدة والدعم للاتحاد!
تشارترز	لم يفيد معهم بعد. إليس أيها كذلك النادل؟
بائع الصحف	لا يعرف. كيف ترتب الأولويات. هذه هي الحقيقة.
تشارترز	كنت كارثة على أعصابك، تعرف له ذلك. إليس؟ سمحت لي أن أكون نذنألذا من الأحد أن أكون واحدًا من يقصدوا. أريد كما أريا كبرذا تحمست لي شيء - حسنا، كان ذلك لك سعيد بذلك وانديا منة كللاغتشاب بالمنة. يبي غحقا.
بائع الصحف	ماذا عن نصف قد فصف حدق آخر - على يلي باسح المحل؟
تشارترز	لم لا لا واحذأت لك النادل، أيها احد يلي حسابي؟
بائع الصحف	لم لا تُشكر نفسك؟
تشارترز	ثانية. نل نتبقاة أشعر بالملامة مع حسن إليس. ليمل جميلق يتعلق هذا ما *(يخرج تشارترز فعله)* أنوى.
بائع الصحف	وستخرج أنت يا كذلك أكن لم إذا يا سيدي *(يخرج إليس).*
	(تشارترز تُغادر العائلة. يربه. يو راقب يفسو راقبًا).
يوسف	هل ترغب في المساعدة يا سيد تشارترز؟
جورج	يسفي. لا يمكنني فعل هذا فتى يا داع لا
يوسف	نعم.
جورج	هذه الملامكة. ة طبيعية دليك ألي كذلك؟
يوسف	فقط انتقاةنتنا ما عادة. هنبه. موطني في للملح حرق.
جورج	وكنت دائمًا تفوز؟
يوسف	لكل مرة.
جورج	من الأفضل أن أشاهد بنفسي إذا؟
يوسف	نعم، فكيف تقول - أنا. أو أكد لهلها السكنة السعادة معك؟
جورج	امسح الأرض.
يوسف	حسنا. كنت أنا الاعتراق بنفسي في إنجلترا. ارا
جورج	كذلك؟ لقد كنت عامل فحم، حسن نعم.
يوسف	لقد ذهبت في رحلة بحرية واحدة فقط.
جورج	لقد كنت بحار قوى ألم تعد لا. المحفم في للعمل رذ عمل هذه كذلك. البنية *(تدخل مارجريت كتشكمش تست ليس).*
مارجريت	هل منها. اشتا آتت تيريت "سترسروديد" في خصيمة لحل رئاتر طفنر نوريين أوانوا كاك أنت بخير يا يسفو؟
يوسف	لكليني شيء ملكوم به.
مارجريت	يمكنك تنقشر ريير بعض البطاطا. انتبه إلى أصل البقعة السلودء.

47

جورج	مارجريت!
مارجريت	آسفة، أنا لم أعن –
يوسف	السيد والسيدة تشارلتون، لقد كان لطفاً كبيراً منكما إيوائي، لكنني أشعر –
جورج	تشعر بماذا يا بني؟
يوسف	أنا لا أعرف ما أشعر به.
مارجريت	ربما يتلاشى ذلك قريباً؟ سينسون كل شيء عنك وبعدها – حسناً.
يوسف	جلبت المشاكل لهذا البيت.
جورج	الآن لا تتحدث أيها الأبله.
يوسف	جلبت المشاكل لثيلما.
مارجريت	أنت تحبها يا بني.
يوسف	بالطبع. أكثر من أي شيء.
مارجريت	حسنا (*دقة على الباب*) من هناك؟
جورج	أنا سأفتح (*يذهب إلى الباب. إنه شرطي*).
الشرطي	آسف لإزعاجك يا جورج. أعتقد أنك تؤوى عندك يوسف عبد الله قريش.
جورج	ماذا؟!
الشرطي	السيد المذكور "قريش" في الحقيقة مهاجر غير شرعي وصدر أمر بترحيله. يجب أن أطلب منك تسليمه إلى السلطات.
جورج	وماذا لو أخبرتك أنه ليس لدي فكرة عما تتحدث؟
الشرطي	إذا يجب أن أخبرك أن عرقلة القانون جريمة يعاقب عليها القانون. وهى إيواء أجنبي بشكل غير قانوني.
جورج	كنت على وشك تناول عشائي، لم لا تغرب عن وجهي؟
الشرطي	جورج لا تصعب الأمر على نفسك.
يوسف	(*يتقدم إلى المدخل*) لا، لا تصعب الأمر على نفسك.
الشرطي	يوسف عبد الله قريش؟ يجب أن أطلب منك مرافقتي إلى مركز الشرطة. آسف على وضع هذه (*يضع الأصفاد*).
يوسف	لا يستطيع الإنسان العيش ككلب مطارد. شكراً لكم. أنتم أناس طيبون.
مارجريت	لكنهم لا يستطيعون أخذك هكذا و–
جورج	أوغاد.
الشرطي	آسف على هذا جورج. فقط أؤدى عملي.
مارجريت	لكن أين سيرسلونه و–
الشرطي	(*يأخذ يوسف بعيدا*) فقط أقوم بعملي (*يخرجون*). بعد بضع ثوان، تدخل ثيلما مسرعة*).
ثيلما	يوسف! قابلت هذا الرجل اليوم، ويقول إن بإمكانه أن يوفر لك عملاً حتى تهدأ الأمور و– (*ثيلما في المشهد*) يوسف؟ يوسف! (*يدخل بائع الصحف ويقرأ من جريدة جازيت*).

48

الرجال الذين تم ترحيلهم ليلة أمس، لم يرتكبوا أى جريمة. قبل الساعة 9.30 تماماً، جاء الرجال الثمانية والثلاثون من سجون مركز الشرطة المركزي. تجاوزوا صفين من ضباط الشرطة، إلى سيارتين من دوريات الشرطة المنتظرة. كانوا يتجهون نحو مدخل البضائع فى محطة السكة الحديدية واصطفوا في نهاية الرصيف. كانوا هادئين للغاية. في الساعة 9.50 تحرك القطار خارج المحطة، وحمل العرب خارج ساوث شيلدز.

النهاية

49